Lowellville, Ohio's Murders, Mayhem and More

Enjoy the Mayhem!

Roslyn Torella

ROSLYN I. TORELLA

DEDICATION

In my memory of my father, David Torella, who inspired me to learn more about the village he proudly called home for nearly eighty-five years.

In memory of my Aunt, Mary Torella Burich Arbie, who once told me that gossip is not a sin… if you are telling the truth.

In memory of my Aunt, Pasqualine Torella Pantana, whose kitchen table I sat around so many times listening to her wonderful stories about Lowellville and its people.

CONTENTS

1 INTRODUCTION

Many of the stories in this book were originally in a manuscript that I put together in 2013 as a gift for my late father, David Torella, to celebrate his eighty-fourth birthday. Since that time many people have encouraged me to publish a book about the history of Lowellville and so I decided to revise the original manuscript and the result is this book.

I have made several updates, added new stories and included information about the incidents that were reported in newspapers from across America. A benefit from researching this book is that I have learned a great deal about the history of my hometown, especially between the decades of the 1850s and the 1920s which are covered in this book.

For many of the stories, I have done additional research about the event or individuals, and where available I have included more information in "historical footnotes". Sometimes I was able to find out what happened after the article was published and at other times it's only the article that is available to tell the story.

One observation is that the early residents of Lowellville were, as a group, hardworking and hard living individuals whose passions sometimes led them into interesting and at times tragic predicaments. I hope that in reading these stories you will find the stories not only entertaining but that the stories will help you experience what life was like during Lowellville's heyday of the late nineteenth and early twentieth centuries.

After spending several years learning about these individuals, they almost feel like family to me and I feel somewhat protective of their legacies, so please do me the favor as you read this book to keep in mind that as human beings they were emotionally complex individuals and these stories are just but one moment in their lifetimes; and these stories could not possibly capture these individuals' true character or essence. It would be unfair to assume that a few lines reported in a newspaper ever could.

Something else to be cognizant of is that Lowellville has a rich immigrant history and as a result many of the individuals who made the newspapers have non-English surnames. You will see a variety of surnames within these pages, and where I was able to determine the actual surname, I have taken the liberty to correct it so that it would be recognizable to the descendants of those individuals who may read this book. When I could not determine the actual surname, I have left it as originally reported. As a result you will see some obviously misspelled surnames.

2 MURDERS AND TRAGIC INCIDENTS

Growing up in Lowellville in the early 1970s through the 1980s, I was familiar with a handful of stories about murders that occurred during the late nineteenth and early twentieth centuries, but it was still hard for me to even imagine that my Lowellville, a sleepy little bedroom town, could have been the setting for some of the events I uncovered while researching this book. You will read stories about unsolved murders, crimes of passion and other sad tragedies. Be warned -- some of the stories in this chapter in particular will leave your heart heavy.

Below is an article that includes a scandal and possible murder from 1855! In the article there was a term I was not familiar with - "grass widow". A "grass widow" is a woman who has been separated from her husband for a long period of time.

The Cincinnati Enquirer *(Cincinnati, OH) published on July 11, 1878:*

OLD BONES

A few days ago the bones of a human male were found in a limestone quarry near Lowellville, this county. This brought to remembrance that twenty-three years ago Aaron Koch suddenly disappeared from Lowellville. Koch had been charged with being criminally intimate with a grass widow named Baker, residing near the quarry. One night a number of masked men went to Baker's residence and took Koch from Mrs. Baker's bed. He was put astride a rail and carried toward the quarry, and has not been heard from since. He was known to have a large amount of money on his person. The leading citizens of Lowellville are investigating the matter, and as some participants in the affair still live in the neighborhood, the excitement is intense.

The next story is about the Cowden Family. The Cowdens were a prominent family in the village, so you can imagine what a stir about the village this sad incident caused...

The New York Times *(New York, NY) published on November 8, 1885:*

SUICIDE OF A DOCTOR'S WIFE

During last night the village of Lowellville, near here, was thrown into great excitement by Dr. J. N. Cowden, the leading physician, rushing into the street stating that his wife had disappeared from his house dressed only in her nightgown. Mrs. Cowden has been so ill for three months as to unsettle her mind. A week ago her husband noticed that she was melancholy, and he placed a close watch over her. He attended her himself at night. Night before last he found her rambling aimlessly about the house. Yesterday afternoon he found her vomiting from the effects of chloroform. She denied taking it, but a two ounce bottle was found under her pillow. The prominence of the doctor caused the whole village to turn out and search for the missing woman. Hundreds of lanterns and torches flitted about in the dark in the search.

A boy said as he crossed the bridge over the river he heard a splash as if someone had fallen in. The crowd, headed by the almost crazy husband, went to the river. The husband spied a white object floating in the water. A boat was manned, and the object proved to be the body of the missing woman. She lay in the water face down, her mass of black hair floating about the face and head. A week ago she asked her husband if he believed a suicide could go to heaven. Though an unbeliever he told her no. A gloom is cast over the whole village, as Mrs. Cowden was highly respected and loved by all who knew her. Mrs. Cowden left the house after sending her attendant to the yard after fresh water. Before leaving the house she took her marriage ring from her finger and left it on the bureau.

Historical Footnote: *The wife was Julia M. Dickinson Cowden and she was born about 1842. She is buried in the Lowellville cemetery. In the 1880 census, the Cowden family included a housekeeper named Agnes Simpson who was a 14 year old Scottish immigrant. Agnes may have been the attendant mentioned in the article. The Cowdens had two sons, their names were Lyman (who was age 14 in 1885) and Charles (who was age 10 in 1885). Her widower, Jasper Newton Cowden remarried in 1887.*

Below are two articles about the tragic death of a pretty Lowellville girl named Annie whose mother arranged "an operation" to protect her daughter's reputation. Sadly, it was the operation that caused the mother to lose the daughter she was trying to protect. Both articles tell essentially the same story but one has more scandalous details than the other and even names the party who caused Annie's "ruin".

The Plain Dealer *(Cleveland, OH) published on September 15, 1886:*

BETRAYED TO DEATH

The sad case of Annie Mohr, Who Died From the Effect of a Criminal Act Performed to Hide Her Shame – Her Mother Confesses the Crime to the Coroner – Cleveland Parties Implicated in the Affair

The body of the late Annie Mohr, who died suddenly at No. 102 Brownwell Street, Cleveland, on Friday last, was brought to Lowellville, this county, on Sunday and buried in the Lowellville cemetery yesterday. The funeral was largely attended, the deceased having formerly lived in Lowellville, where she had a multitude of friends and acquaintances.

Coroner West of Cleveland

Late last night accompanied by Dr. J. F. Armstrong, Coroner West went to the cemetery armed with a permit from the township trustees and exhumed the body. A post mortem examination was made and evidences gleaned pointing to abortion as the cause of death.

A Criminal Operation

Mrs. Sophia Mohr, the mother of the deceased girl, confessed to the coroner that a criminal operation had been performed over two weeks ago by Dr. C. G. Ashley of Cleveland, for a fee of $150. She said she learned of her daughter's unfortunate condition about four weeks ago and set about to save her reputation, if possible. Drs. Carpenter and Hawkins were called upon first, but they refused to touch the case; Ashley consented, and the girl who had been clerking in the dry goods store of O. D. Myers & Co., recovered sufficiently to accept a position in a Cleveland store, but a relapse set in and on the day she first went to work she was taken ill and retuned home, where she died Friday morning.

Mrs. Mohr told the Coroner that John F. Denham of the firm Denham & Smith, hardware merchants in Cleveland, had caused the girl's ruin. The coroner took portions of the body and Mrs. Mohr's deposition to Cleveland to be turned over to the authorities. Mrs. Mohr is a cripple from rheumatism and is the sister of H. D. Smith, the postmaster at Lowellville. She has been divorced from her husband, Jacob Mohr, for over ten years. When Annie was a mere child they lived in Sharon where Mr. Mohr had a large mercantile store. One night the store burned out and Mohr suddenly disappeared and nothing has been seen of him since, although he is believed to be somewhere in the south. About five years ago Mrs. Mohr and Annie moved to Greenville, Pa, and from there to Cleveland. When a school girl at Lowellville, Annie was vivacious and very pretty.

Here is the second article published in **The Cleveland Leader** *(Cleveland, OH) on September 15, 1886:*

ANNA MOHR
A Post Mortem Examination Held by the Light of a Lantern – The Mother's Statement

Coroner West returned from Lowellville, Mahoning county, yesterday morning where he succeeded in holding a post-mortem examination of the body of Anna Mohr, with the assistance of Dr. J. F. Armstrong. When the Coroner arrived at Lowellville he found that his telegram relative to the exhuming the body had not been delivered. Miss Mohr was buried at noon and it was after 9 o'clock in the evening when Coroner West succeeded in obtaining permission to disinter the body. Before the remains were removed from the grave, a large number of people assembled and would have caused trouble had the Coroner not demonstrated his authority. The body was carried into a tool shanty, and by the fitful glare of a lantern the post mortem was held. The result showed very conclusively that a criminal operation had been resorted to, and such will be Dr. Armstrong's report to the Coroner.

Yesterday morning Coroner West called upon Mrs. Mohr, the mother of the dead girl. She at first denied that anything wrong had been done, but when the Coroner told her of the post mortem, she broke completely down and acknowledged that a criminal operation has been committed. "I am as guilty as anyone else," said she, "but it was to save my daughter from disgrace." Those present at the interview deny that Mrs. Mohr said the operation was performed to save her girl's life. Mrs. Mohr stated that a St. Clair street doctor came to the house at one time and that after he left Anna told her he had come for the purpose of operating on her, but she refused to let him do so unless he would give her chloroform. Several days later, the doctor who performed the operation came, but Mrs. Mohr was not present and could only state what she inferred took place in the bedroom.

A woman living on St. Clair street says Anna Mohr told her that the St. Clair street doctor operated on her, but the physician Mrs. Mohr believes to have been implicated lives on the West Side. The time that the crime is alleged to have been committed was about the middle of August. Dr. West is unable to state whether or not any criminal prosecutions will follow, but yet no positive testimony has been obtained against any one. Mrs. Mohr states that the young man whose name has figured extensively in the case knew nothing of the matter, except that he sent her $30 when he learned of the girl's illness and $20 after her death to assist in defraying the funeral expenses.

Historical Footnote: *Annie's mother was the sister of the village's first Mayor H.D. Smith. The physician named in the article as performing Annie's abortion was still practicing medicine after 1885, therefore I assume he was never criminally convicted as an accessory to her death. As for a little bit about Annie - shortly, before her death, I found a mention in a Cleveland, Ohio newspaper that reported that she had been accused of stealing a parasol from a local merchant. So apparently Annie was a bit of a rebel for her time.*

Probably the village's most strangest tale of death is that of thirty-five year old Jess Allshouse , here is the story of his very unusual drowning...

The New Castle News *(New Castle, PA) published on March 30, 1898:*

DROWNED IN SHALLOW WATER
Jess Allshouse Meets Death in Rather a Peculiar Manner

Jess Allshouse, a well-known resident of Lowellville, O., was drowned shortly before the noon hour Monday by falling into an open culvert while walking along the P. & L. E. tracks and a short distance east of the station in Lowellville. The culvert is only about two feet deep and the water at the bottom in which Allshouse drowned was not more than two and one half inches deep. It is thought that he was intoxicated and in walking along the track he stumbled, falling into the culvert head first. He was evidently stunned by the fall, and his face being in the water, he was drowned before returning to consciousness which could have given him the strength to save himself. Allshouse was 35 years old and had been employed by the furnace in Lowellville. He was unmarried and resided with his mother.

On a beautiful spring day two little girls while out picking flowers discovered the body of a "John Doe" whose only known identity appears to have been unlucky "Number 13":

The New Castle News *(New Castle, PA) published on April 23, 1902:*

FOUND WITH HIS SKULL FRACTURED

The body of an unknown man was found east of Lowellville, Mahoning county, yesterday afternoon and there is every indication that he was murdered. Coroner Blott, who was called to make an investigation last night informed **The Vindicator** reporter this morning that he believes a murder was committed.

The crime, he says, may have been committed many weeks or perhaps months ago. It is possible that the foul act may have been committed months ago, probably as far back as last fall.

The ghastly discovery was made by the two Burkey girls, who live not far from the woods where the body was found. The little ones took advantage of the beautiful spring day and started from home shortly after dinner to gather flowers. After wandering through the woods and fields for a time they finally went upon the property owned by Mrs. Henry Miller. The property is located just about two and one half miles from the village of Lowellville and not far from Hillsville.

It was the in the woods of the Miller property that the body was found. Badly frightened, the two girls hastened home and told their father of the discovery they made. Mr. Burkey notified a number of the neighbors of the story told by his children and they all started for the woods where the body lay. Upon their arrival there they found the report by the two children only too true. The body was found in the thickest part of the woods, it was in almost a kneeling posture, and the head was literally buried in the leaves. The leaves had either blown about the head or else the murderer, or murderers, had piled them there. There was a terrible stench owing to its decomposed condition, and Mr. Burkey and the others in the party were wild about making an investigation, but they succeeded far enough with their examination to convince them that a terrible crime had been committed.

It was not until 8 o'clock last night that a message was sent from Lowellville to Coroner Blott, and he at once repaired to the place where the body lay. He ordered the body removed to the morgue of Cunningham and Davidson in Lowellville, and before he returned home, he performed the unpleasant duty of holding a post mortem examination. The post mortem revealed that the unknown man had undoubtedly been struck a terrible blow with an instrument of some kind, for the skull was fractured, death probably resulting from that cause. The forehead was badly bruised, there was a bad cut on the left side of the cheek, a scalp wound besides, and an awful cut in the head, which had been afflicted when the skull was fractured.

The skull was fractured at the roof. In the pockets of the clothes worn by the dead man was found 16 cents, a dime, a nickel and a penny, a time book and a string of rosary beads. There was nothing written in the time book that would have a tendency to disclose the identity of the dead man. There was written in the Slovenian language the words "I have worked", and below these words were the figures "168" in two different places. On the first page of the book were the figures "13" in a number of places. There was nothing else written in the book.

Coroner Blott in an interview this morning said, "There is no doubt in my mind but what the man was murdered, and the crime may have been committed as far back as last fall. The head lay in a pool of blood, which was still moist owing to the fact that the head was covered over and buried in a pile of leaves, so it is hard to say how long the body has been in the woods, or when the crime was committed. There is every indication and evidence of murder, and at this late date it will be a hard matter to find the guilty party."

The following legal notice of the finding of the body was received today at *The Vindicator* office from Coroner Blott:

To Whom It May Concern:

An unknown man, aged about 35, dark brown hair, brown eyes, light brown mustache, wearing a black coat, black trousers, blue cap, no vest, suit of gray cotton underwear and lace shoes. He also wore a leather belt with a brass buckle. The victim was a man about 5 feet 5 inches and weighed about 150 pounds, one of his front teeth was broken off. He had in his possession a small account book with No. 13 written on the first page, small looking glass, comb, a string of rosary beads and 16 cents in money. He was killed in some unknown manner and was found in the woods of the Mrs. Henry Miller farm on the state line road about two and one half miles from Lowellville. DR. H.E. BLOTT, Coroner

The belief that the victim of the supposed tragedy was a Slovenian and the minute description of the victim furnished by Coroner Blott may lead to identification, provided the victim was Slovenian. In that event all the Slovenians in the valley will take a personal interest in the case, as they always do, and will unquestionably throw some light on the case.

Historical Footnote: The identity of Number 13 was never discovered and his murderer or murderers never brought to justice. His unclaimed body was laid to rest in the Lowellville cemetery's potter's field. Perhaps there was a family back in Slovenia who wondered what had happened to their loved one. As for there being no name in his account book, it was not uncommon for quarry or mill workers to keep track of their hours of work in books such as the one found on the victim. In this time period, some employers simply identified their employees by a number rather than a name because they had no legal or business need to record much personal information about their employees as there were no payroll withholdings or wage reporting requirements as there are today.

Here are two articles related to a grisly murder that took place in Lowellville in the spring of 1913. The murder weapon was an adz which is an axe like tool used by railroad workers. The two murdered men were part of a work crew stationed in Lowellville to repair the railroad tracks damaged by the big March 1913 flood. Even stranger than the actual murder, was a letter Lowellville's Marshal Tony Fisher received from the alleged murderer.

The New Castle News *(New Castle, PA) published on April 22, 1913:*

DOUBLE MURDER IN LOWELLVILLE VILLAGE; SLAYER STILL AT LARGE
Two Men Killed As Fiend Wields Adz in Box Car
Cuts Victims to Ribbons With Deadly Weapon and Makes His Escape
Blood Hounds Lose the Scent
Dogs Baffled by Reason of Tracks Made by Curious Who Gathered at Scene

Two men were murdered some time during last night in the foulest crime that has ever occurred in this vicinity.

One of the men, Frank Starci, was cut to pieces, and the other was so badly mutilated that he died on the way to the Youngstown City Hospital.

The men had been set upon by some unknown fiend with an adz. After knocking them down in a Baltimore & Ohio box car, he proceeded to chop them to ribbons.

The murder was discovered at 4 o'clock this morning. The men, both Polanders, were employed by the Baltimore & Ohio Railroad company on construction work, and occupied one of the cars that was used in transporting construction gangs from one place to the other.

Thought It Was Duel

When the car was broken into after the bloody adz had been found on the outside, it was the first idea that the crime was the result of a duel between the two men, but a subsequent investigation showed that the men had been foully murdered.

The finding of the adz on the outside proved that the crime had been committed by someone who had thrown the weapon to one side as he hurriedly escaped.

Bloodhounds were brought here but they were unable to take the scent owing to the fact that scores had tramped about the cars before the hounds arrived.

Killed While Asleep

The unfortunate men may have been killed while they slept, for there were no signs of a struggle in the car.

When the car was opened and other members of the construction gang hurriedly entered, an awful sight met their gaze. Starci was lying on the floor of the car. He was literally chopped to pieces. He was one mass of blood and was dead.

His companion, whose name is unknown, was still alive. He had been cut in a horrible manner by swift strokes of the adz, which was as sharp as a razor. He died on the way to the hospital without gaining consciousness.

The police of Lowellville and the county officials are working on the case, but they do not have a single clue that would enable them to arrest the murderer. Several suspects were jailed, but they were released after an examination. No reason for the crime could be given.

Here is the article about the letter published in the **New Castle News** *(New Castle, PA) on May 2, 1913:*

NOTE CONFESSES BOX CAR MURDERS
Lowellville Marshal Receives Message to Release Suspects Held for Crime

Marshal Fisher received on Thursday morning a letter written on a portion of a Cleveland paper of April 20. It reads as follows:

"Der Sir:

"This is to tel you I am going far away an ther aint no use for you to held them Guys you have down ther. I am the guy that done the job inn the kar an ther aint no use to look for me."

A blue pencil was used and a pair of daggers crossing each other were the only marks indicating a signature.

The "guys" referred to are the ten men who were held as suspects in the recent box car murder. They have already been released.

Historical footnote: The ten men initially held as suspects were the other men on the construction gang. Within a few days after the discovery of the victims an unusual theory began to unfold. There was no blood outside of the boxcar and the weapon was actually found inside the car lying near Revitch, the name of the second victim. There had been a pile of adzes lying in the corner of the boxcar. It was evident that the men had been drinking heavily, as a case of beer bought the day of the murders was just about gone. Was it possible that the two men had killed each other? Revitch was tall at 6 foot and a strong man and Starci was of a medium build. Starci received a strong blow to the head which killed him and Revitch had terrible facial wounds with his lower jaw almost severed to the ear from a blow across the face with the adz. The final theory of the case emerged— during a booze induced argument between the two, it was believed that Starci grabbed an adz from the pile and struck Revitch across the face and with adrenaline rushing through him, Revitch took the adz from Starci and struck him in the head, killing him. Revitch suffering from a loss of blood, fell back onto his bunk and lay there dying - too weak to summon help. No family or friends came to claim their remains and both were buried in the Lowellville cemetery's potter's field.

This next article makes you wonder if this was really a case of mistaken identity or a father protecting the innocence of his young daughter ...

The Youngstown Vindicator *(Youngstown, OH) published December 30, 1915:*

FANDOZZI HOME IS UNDER GUARD
Lowellville Police Protect Man Who Killed Daughter's Lover

Lowellville police authorities acting under instructions from the prosecutor's office Wednesday night placed a guard about the home of Mike Fandozzi, near the Ohio-Pennsylvania state line. Fandozzi last Saturday night shot and killed Joe Fascio alias Fisher, whom it is claimed had tried to force an entrance into the Fandozzi home to abduct Mary Fandozzi, aged 12 years old.

Tuesday evening an attempt was made to pry a window at the Fandozzi residence. It is thought that those seeking to gain an entrance had designs on the life of Fandozzi. The matter was reported to the Lowellville authorities who in turn consulted with the prosecutor. In order to forestall any plot to kill the man who did the shooting, it was thought best to place the home under guard. The officer was instructed to arrest any person making suspicious moves about the place.

Terms of endearment dictated by an unwilling heart and written in a trembling hand under a compelling fear of a violent death.

It is alleged, are contained in a letter written by Mary Fandozzi, aged 12, to Joe Fascio alias Fisher, 23 years old. The letter is now in possession of County Detective John J. Kane.

Fascio, alias Fisher, was shot and killed Saturday night by Mike Fandozzi, father of the girl. The details of the shooting have already been published in the **Vindicator**. Fandozzi it is claimed mistook Fascio for burglar.

All parties are Italians living below Lowellville close to the Ohio-Pennsylvania state line. Fascio was in love with the little girl. Last week he called on Mary and declared that he meant to abduct her. He warned her that if she told her parents she would meet a violent death. Before leaving Fascio secured a promise from the child that she would write him a letter in which she would state how much she loved him. He gave her the number of his post office box at Lowellville. Mary forgot the number of the box and for that reason did not mail the letter which she had written. Fascio called at the Fandozzi home last Friday evening and Mary handed him the letter, which was found in his pocket after he had been killed.

The letter was written with pencil on a sheet of writing paper. The writer asked Fascio and his brother to spend Christmas at her home. She declared that she loved Fascio and did not care who knew that fact. At the end just before her signature appears several X marks beneath which is the explanation, "These are meant for kisses."

On the following night, Fandozzi heard someone trying to force up one of the windows. He secured a shotgun and went to the kitchen door. In the faint light he discerned a man running towards the hills. He fired one shot in the air and the man stopped and started back towards to the house.

When he was about 40 feet away, Fandozzi let go with the shot gun. The charge struck Fascio in the breast instantly killing him. When Fandozzi saw the face of his victim he was frantic with grief. Lowellville Officers found a murderous looking butcher knife in Fascio's coat pocket. The butcher knife, similar to one found on Fascio, is missing from his boarding house. It is thought he armed himself with the knife before going to the Fandozzi home.

Historical Footnote*: The victim's surname was reported as Mascio, but on his death certificate it was shown as Fascio. The surname Fascio is similar sounding to his alias of Fisher. Fandozzi was never convicted of Fascio's murder.*

3 TALES OF LOVE AND SOME GONE WRONG

The stories in this chapter are probably some of my favorites because they show how affairs of the heart can lead individuals to situations that range from the scandalous to the downright humorous.

Apparently a young Lowellville man in 1878 was quite the lover and the local gals were quite gullible…

The Cincinnati Enquirer *(Cincinnati, OH) published on January 4, 1878:*

YOUNGSTOWN, OHIO, NEWS

Today the County Infirmary Directors met in Lowellville, this county, to take charge of five girls, all about eighteen years of age and unmarried, who are about to become mothers. It is alleged that one young man of a good family is the author of the shame of three of the girls.

Who doesn't love an elopement story? This 1878 account was published in several newspapers in the United States and as far away as Australia.

The Mercury and Weekly Courier *(Fitzroy, Victoria, Australia) published on December 28, 1878:*

A WEDDING ON THE WATER
A Young Couple from Ohio Circumvent a Hard Hearted Parent

There was a funny little wedding on the 4th of July on one of the steamers on the Schuylkill, above the waterworks. It was a wedding in which flowers, presents and bridal retinue played no part, although its pretty safe to say that the parties concerned are of social standing and well to do in the world's affairs. Whoever had been on board the steamer Rockland has noticed the little space abaft the retiring rooms. It is scarcely as large as the platform of a streetcar, and four people standing up will occupy all the space. It required only three persons to complete the ceremony in question. One was the preacher, Rev. Dallas Mays, of Lowellville, Mahoning Co., O., a town on the Youngstown and Ashtabula branch of the Pittsburgh, Fort Wayne and Chicago Railroad, forty-three miles from Pittsburgh. The other two were Miss Fannie Doud, a daughter of Dr. Doud, a dentist in the same village where the reverend gentleman above named expounds the Scriptures from the holy desk of the Presbyterian Church. The third party to this matrimonial transaction was Mr. James Powers, of Poland, O., a town not far from Lowellville, where he carried on the business of a wool-merchant. He is young in years, handsome in person and of a romantic turn. His business association with Dr. Doud, the dentist, has not been pleasant, and a love engagement that had grown up between the young people when the father and the lover were on amicable terms, was declared off when the amity between the two ceased to exist. The old gentleman's voice had no weight in such a matter as this, and the young couple continued on the path leading to their mutual happiness despite orders, threats and remonstrances.

Now this story is based upon the statement of Mr. Powers, made in the presence of Mrs. Powers, nee Doud, who gave nodding confirmation of the narration as it progressed; therefore, whosoever reflects upon the hard-heartedness of Mr. Doud grows out of the endorsed assertion of the newly-made husband. The parent denied the lover admission to the house, but she, upon the pretext of visiting friends in Pittsburgh, met Powers there (he was her friend indeed) and together they came to Philadelphia, arriving on a the train which deposits travelers from the West at the Market Street depot at 7:35am. Mr. Mays had gone East to attend the alumni meeting at Princeton, his Alma Mater, and by preconcerted arrangement he had remained East until the young couple came on. They were to have been married in the evening at the Lafayette Hotel, where they were stopping, but the trio visiting Fairmount Park, and all the parties willing, the knot was quietly tied on the boat just as she passed under two bridges at Girard Avenue. They supped at the Belmont. Mr. Mays went back to his church, and the 4 o'clock train yesterday to Cape May took the newly-married romantic couple to the Stockton House.

Here is a story about compensating a lady for her "ruin" in exchange for dismissing a charge of bastardly against her former lover. This scandal was apparently cleared up with a onetime payment so that both parties could go on with their lives... well at least the party who had no evidence of "ruin" so readily apparent.

The Cleveland Leader *(Cleveland, OH) published on December 18, 1884:*

A sensation was occasioned today by Miss Lizzie M. Allen, a pretty young milliner engaged in business on East Federal Street, swearing out a warrant for the arrest of Calvin Reeder Jr., of Lowellville, this county, on a charge of bastardy. Miss Allen came here a year ago from Plaingrove, PA and opened a millinery store. Being handsome, and possessing excellent taste to please the ladies, she soon secured a large custom, and the revelation today was something unexpected by her many friends. Miss Allen alleged that her ruin was accomplished under promise of marriage, and as the accused, Reeder, who is a young man living with his father in Lowellville, was brought to the city in charge of an officer. A conference was held and a settlement was effected, the accused paying a sufficient sum of money to induce the complainant to dismiss the case.

Historical Footnote: *Lizzie gave birth to a baby boy, returned to Pennsylvania where she married a different man who raised her child and gave the child his surname.*

Here is another sad story that was quite scandalous in 1886.

The Cincinnati Commercial Tribune *(Cincinnati, OH) published on May 15, 1886:*

A VITAL VICTIM

Nearly everyone in the village of Struthers six miles from here attended the funeral of Mattie Smith, a young colored girl today. The girl who was about nineteen years old, was reared in Struthers, and had always borne a good humor. About three months ago she went to Pittsburgh, and her parents supposed she was working there as a domestic.

Later developments prove that she was stopping at a cheap boarding house, her expenses being paid by a white man from Lowellville, who is about thirty-five years old, two weeks ago the girl gave birth to a girl baby, nearly white. When she began sinking she sent for her sister, who resides in

Struthers, and to her disclosed the secret of her ruin. At the same time Mattie gave her the key to her trunk wherein were kept the letters of her betrayer. From these it was learned that, to accomplish his design, the man represented to Mattie that he was wealthy and would give her certain pieces of property.

When Mattie was asked by her sister why she left home, she said it was her intention to never return to Struthers and bring disgrace upon her parents. It is thought that want of proper care caused the girl's death, the child is still living. The man whom the dead girl charged with being her betrayer is Frank Meeker, well known throughout the neighborhood. He has departed from Lowellville. The people of Lowellville express great indignation over the affair.

Historical Footnote: Frank Meeker, the alleged father, was a thirty-five year old store clerk, certainly not a wealthy man who owned a large amount of real estate as he led poor Mattie to believe.

This next story brings to mind the saying "Hell hath no fury like a woman scorned"...

The Cleveland Leader *(Cleveland, OH) published on July 13, 1887:*

Mrs. Barbara Frank, a middle aged widow residing in Petersburg, this county, came here today and caused the arrest of Fred Barser, of Lowellville. The buxom widow stated that Barser courted her for a year and they were engaged to be married when another woman stepped in and secured the matrimonial prize. The widow met Barser yesterday and on unbraiding him for his actions, she alleges he struck her with his fist.

Harry Belafonte's lyrics ring so true in this little story - "If you wanna be happy for the rest of your life, never make a pretty woman your wife. So from my personal point of view, get an ugly girl to marry you."

The Repository *(Canton, OH) published on October 3, 1889:*

HOW A MAHONING COUNTY MAN WAS DECEIVED BY A

YOUNGSTOWN COURTESAN

Two weeks ago Patterson Reed, a real estate owner residing at Lowellville, this county, visited this city and made his acquaintance of Cora Eastman, an inmate of a disreputable house. He fell in love with the fair Cora and asked her to become his wife. She consented, and it was agreed that Cora was to go to Lowellville and the marriage would take place Monday evening. The beguiled Lowellite secured a marriage license, and the house he was to occupy he furnished and invited a number of friends to witness the ceremony. When the groom arrived, the prospective bride was not forthcoming, and it was then that Reed realized he has been sold. The girl said she never intended to marry the man, and she said was only "guying" him.

Here are two articles that were published in **The Plain Dealer** *(Cleveland, OH) a few weeks apart in 1891 that are related to one another. The altercation that is described in the first article, probably was talked about in town for some time…*

Published on February 7, 1891:

A FIGHT BETWEEN FATHERS
The Parent of the Betrayed Girl Thrashes the Father of her Alleged Seducer

This morning Porter Watson and John Grist, two of Lowellville's best known and respected citizens, got into a fight as they were waiting for an early train at the Pittsburgh & Lake Erie depot at Lowellville to bring them to this city. Watson is a well-known furnace man and Grist is a wealthy farmer. The cause of the trouble is the old story of "loving not wisely but too well" by Watson's pretty daughter and Grist's youngest son. Night before last, Watson's unmarried daughter gave birth to a child and young Grist is said to be its father. The young man several weeks ago was perfectly willing to marry the girl but his father would not have it and sent his son away. Watson at the time was away on business and did not know of his daughter' trouble. As soon as Mrs. Watson learned of it, she telegraphed him and he came home. When he learned that young Grist had left, he took the train in the same direction and spent ten days looking for the young man who had deceived his lovely daughter but returned without finding him.

This morning Watson stepped up to Grist and asked if his son was going to do the right thing by his daughter. Grist replied: "I would have my son marry your daughter before night, if I was sure my son was the father of your daughter's child." This was more than Watson could stand, and he let drive with his right fist and knocked Grist sprawling to the platform. He then jumped on him to administer some more of the same treatment, when bystanders interfered and held Watson in check. Both men took the train and came here. Grist called upon a physician and had his eye and nose dressed. Grist is the older of the two. Both families stand high and move in the best society. The affair has a created a big sensation in this vicinity.

Historical Footnote: *Porter's daughter, Mary Watson, gave birth to a baby boy on February 6, 1891 and named him Bert Grist. Mary and Bert's father never married and went on to marry others.*

This second article published a few weeks later on March 13, 1891, makes mention of the Watson-Grist fight proving that spicy stories take a long time to fade in small towns:

A DOMESTIC SUES A MAYOR
Miss Mary Jane Burke of Lowellville Asks for $10,000 of Mayor Smith for Alleged Slander

The Mayor of Lowellville, Henry D. Smith, has been sued by Mary Jane Burke, a domestic in the employ of D. E. Webster, the druggist of that town, for the sum of $10,000 in damages for alleged slander. The slander complained of by the plaintiff is a remark alleged to have been made by Smith that Miss Burke and Webster would furnish a greater sensation than that made there recently by the Watson and Grist disclosures. The young woman alleges in her petition that the defendant meant by his remark that she was unchaste and had been living unlawfully intimate with Druggist Webster. The plaintiff says she is an unmarried woman of good character and that her good name has been damaged.

This article describes a court hearing involving an 18 year old Lowellville man named Clark Cramer. Clark was accused of trying to convince his 21 year old girlfriend to abort their unborn child by ingesting a "medicine" commonly used for that purpose.

The Youngstown Vindicator *(Youngstown, OH) published on July 16, 1892:*

SEVERE CHARGES

Made In a Case That is Now on Trial
With Severe Penalties Attached
If the Charges are Found, Finally True - Circumstances of the Case
The case of Ohio vs Clark Cramer was called in Squire Hellawell's court this morning.

The case is a very disgusting one and much of the testimony is unfit for publication.

A few weeks ago Miss Lizzie Townley, of Struthers, had the defendant in the present case arrested on a charge of betrayal. In the trial he was bound over to court by a Lowellville justice. It was during this trial that the plaintiff was severely cross-examined, and to further make her charges good against Cramer she produced medicine after the trial which she alleged had been given to her to take by the defendant.

A warrant was then issued by Squire Hellawell and Cramer was arrested and the case set for this morning. Miss Townley was represented by Attorney Jacobs, while the interest of the boy were attended by J. S. Roller. During the trial the defendant sat near his father and attempted to keep up his spirits by nervously playing with his hat. During the cross examination of the witnesses, his face was wreathed in smiles.

The first witness called was T. R. McEwen, the druggist. He was shown the package and the bottle of medicine which Cramer is said to have given the girl to take.

He stated that both medicines were classed as emensgogues, but beyond this his testimony was not of importance.

Mrs. Mary Davis was the next witness called. She was a clever talker and kept the court laughing by her quick retorts to Attorney Roller when the latter attempted to catch her up in her testimony. She said she lived on East Federal Street and her testimony about that as follows:

"Have known Lizzie Townley twelve years; knew the whole family; her mother is dead; her father is again married and lives at Wheatland; I saw that young man at my house two weeks ago. (Pointing at Cramer)

"He said to me; 'What is the least you will take and keep the girl.' I told him $3 a week was the least I could afford to keep her for. He said he wanted her kept at my house so it would keep down the suspicion, and on the Fourth of July he would marry her. I went ahead and made

21

arrangements for the wedding. He asked me if she had taken the medicine. I said: No, I have it in my care. He told me he gave the medicine to the girl, but did not tell me what for, as I knew that myself. I told him that if she took the medicine and anything should happen, I would not be responsible for it. She was compelled to leave home on account of Cramer, as her brother, with whom she was staying, did not want her to keep company with him."

Attorney Jacobs then handed her the medicine and asked her if she had seen it before. She said "yes sir, that is the same medicine that he gave her. I told Lizzie not to take it, as I knew what it would do."

Upon being cross examined by Mr. Roller, she said: "I gave the medicine to Lizzie afterwards to take to Mr. Jacobs. It is the same medicine. She went to her brother's to stay because her stepmother was cruel to her. Her brother turned her out because she would not stop going with Cramer. Never heard she was a bad girl. She is now living with me."

Mr. Roller here asked the witness if the girl had ever been in Alice Hall's resort on East Federal street. She replied, "No sir; but once, and I went with her to see somebody. Do not know what kind of house she keeps. If you know what kind of a house she keeps all right, I don't. I have heard the girl called Blinkey Morgan."

After a few quick retorts with the attorney, Mrs. Davis was allowed to retire and the plaintiff was called. Her testimony in regard to who she was and where she lived corroborated with that given by Mrs. Davis.

In regard to meeting Cramer she said: "I met him near my sister's house; We were introduced; I have known him since April; I am now in a delicate condition and he is responsible for it; I told him about it and he asked me if I had a place to go and would pay my board.

"I spoke with Mrs. Davis and then told him I could stay there for $3 a week. I met him before this and we had some words and I said I would have him arrested; he said no, don't do that, I'll pay your board and care for the child."

She was here shown the medicine and told how she had received it.

She said: "Cramer said he would get me some stuff to take. I told him I would not. He then said he would get it anyhow and he went to Niles the next morning after it. When he got back he handed me the stuff and said, will you take it. I said no. He said, it's no use giving it to you then. I said, oh you might as well, but I won't take it. The package contained directions but I can't read. He read them, but I paid no attention."

The case was then paused until 1 o'clock this afternoon.

The case was continued again this afternoon. A motion to dismiss the case was over-ruled by the squire, and the defendant was bound over to common pleas court in the sum of $250.

The girl in the case is 21 years old, while the defendant is several years her junior.

Historical Footnote: The young woman in this case, Elizabeth "Lizzie" Townley, refused to take the drug and eventually gave birth on February 8, 1893 to a little girl named Sarah Cramer in Struthers, Ohio. Clark died at the age of 24 on January 9, 1899 of typhoid fever in Struthers, Ohio and was buried in the Lowellville cemetery. At the time of his death his he was unmarried and he was employed as a telegraph operator in Wheeling, West Virginia.

Lizzie married a different man in 1898 and her daughter took this man's surname. Lizzie lived to age 70 and she, like Clark, is buried in the Lowellville cemetery.

The name of "Blinkey Morgan" is in reference to the alias used by a man named Charles Conklin, who with two others in 1887, stole a large quantity of valuable furs from a Cleveland, Ohio store. When attempting to capture "Morgan" at his headquarters in Michigan, a shootout occurred and a sheriff was shot and killed. "Morgan" was found guilty and hanged.

Now for something a little lighter ... I was surprised to see this small article containing such salacious gossip printed in the newspaper ...

The New Castle News *(New Castle, PA) published on April 10, 1895:*

WHO WERE THEY?

A Lowellville special today says, "A young woman from Youngstown and a man from New Castle, names not known, met here by appointment yesterday and stopped over night at one of the hotels here, before leaving for their respective homes this morning. Woman, brunette, about 25 years old. Man, brown mustache, about 35 years old.

Here is another scandalous incident that I am sure had "tongues wagging" about town ...

I do want to note that I found it odd that the man accused of assault in this story, Thomas Driscoll, talked about the snakes he killed and equally strange was that the reporter who wrote this story found it interesting enough to include in his report. I guess in 1895, big black snakes were a big deal.

The Youngstown Vindicator *(Youngstown, OH) published on April 23, 1895:*

APPREHENDED
Thomas Driscoll Will Have to Answer a Criminal Charge He Had Assaulted a Woman
A Wealthy Young Farmer Arraigned Last Night - He Tells a Snake Story

Thomas Driscoll, a young farmer residing near Lowellville, was arrested by Constable Richard Morgan at 5 o'clock last evening, on a very serious charge.

Mrs. Della O. Rentz, who resides on a farm near Lowellville, was on her way home from that village on the evening of April 8. Her way led past the farm occupied by the Driscolls, and according to her story while passing a field in which Thomas Driscoll was plowing, he jumped over the fence into the road, stopped her and made an indecent proposal.

Mrs. Rentz repulsed him indignantly, whereupon Driscoll took hold of her and attempted to drag her from the road. The woman resisted and almost had the clothes torn from her person. The timely appearance of Mr. Rentz, her husband, Mrs. Rentz claims, prevented Driscoll from accomplishing his base purpose. Driscoll hurriedly left the scene, leaving his horses standing in the field.

The above story was told by Mr. and Mrs. Rentz the day following the assault to Squire Reilly, who immediately issued a warrant for Driscoll charging him with assault with attempt to rape. The warrant was placed in the hands of Constable Morgan, who until yesterday did not have an opportunity of serving it. The constable went to Lowellville and walked out to Driscoll's place and found the young man plowing in the field, part of which is in Pennsylvania and part in Ohio. Driscoll either did not know who the constable was, or did not care for he made no attempt to get away, and when told what he was wanted for, made no resistance and accompanied the officer to the city.

Driscoll was arraigned before Justice Reilly about 8 o'clock last evening, and pleaded not guilty. The squire fixed Driscoll's bond at $500, which was signed by Daniel A. Davidson, of Lowellville. Driscoll's hearing will take place Tuesday, April 30, at 9 o'clock a.m.

On his way to this city with the constable, Driscoll said that during the day while plowing he had killed several blacksnakes in the field, the smallest of which was over five feet long. He said his horses would go along all right until they got scent of a snake, when they would refuse to go father until the driver hunted up the reptile, and killed it. These incidents, he said, occurred frequently during his day's work. He claimed to be able to prove his innocence of the criminal charge.

Historical Footnote: Thomas Driscoll eventually became a Lowellville police officer and around 1915 he moved from Lowellville to Warren Ohio and lived there until his death at age 65 in December 1940. He and his wife, Catherine Baughman Driscoll, had two children, Thomas and Helen. Cora "Della" Taylor Rentz remained in Lowellville and died at the age of 91 on December 14, 1969.

Here's a story that appears to have a happy ending, but life does not always go as planned as you will discover in the footnote to this story…

The Plain Dealer *(Cleveland, OH) published on November 30, 1895:*

THEY WERE BEATEN AGAIN
Efforts of Lovers to Get Married Repeatedly Frustrated by the Girl's Vigilant Father

Cyrus Cramer and Miss Maud May of Lowellville are having a serious time trying to get married. They have left home several times determined to have the nuptial knot tied, but each time their plans have been frustrated by the young lady's father, who very strongly objects to Cramer as a son-in-law.

Cramer has been twice married, and it is not secret that both of his wives left him because he failed to provide for them to their satisfaction.

The last attempt of Cramer and Miss May to get married was made today, but they told some of their friends of their intention and before they left Lowellville, May heard of it. He drove post haste to this city and warned the probate judge not to issue a marriage license with his daughter's name on it, as she is not yet of age. Of course Cramer and his would be bride were very much disappointed, but they consoled themselves by concluding to return home and try again in a few days.

Historical Footnote: Maud and Cyrus did eventually marry. They went to Portage County and were married on December 4, 1895 with Maud giving her residence as Rootstown, Ohio. In the 1900 Census I found Cyrus, who was 29 years old and living with his in-laws Elias and Amanda May along with his 3 year old son Charles Cramer, who was born in December 1896. Sadly Maud had died sometime between 1899 and July 1900. The details are sketchy but I discovered that she was killed in a train accident. In an article about the death of her brother-in-law, Chauncey Cramer, who was killed when he fell off a train he had hitched a ride on, the reporter wrote that Chauncey's sister-in-law (our Maud) was killed in a similar accident a few months earlier at the Pennsylvania crossing in Haselton. Unfortunately, I was not able to find the article about Maud's death. This is just a sad story, nonetheless it seems that Cyrus eventually does find happiness. Cyrus married for the fourth time around 1906 and he and his wife were together until Cyrus' death in 1925.

This next story about bigamy may surprise you but bigamy was not uncommon in the early twentieth century, because it was far easier to run away and start a new life than to get to divorced. Additionally, for immigrants it could get pretty lonely in a new country when your spouse was still back home across the ocean. I am guessing that its possible that Lorenzo's wife was still in Italy. I am at a loss as to exactly what Antonia's motivation was, except, perhaps she was just trying to find a good man.

The Youngstown Vindicator (Youngstown, OH) published on January 21, 1902:

MUCHLY MARRIED WOMAN
Mayor Vogan of Lowellville Hands Out a Salty Dose to a Bad Pair

Lorenzo Marsocci and Mrs. Antonia Diana, arrested last Saturday, and confined in the county jail to await trial on a charge of bigamy, were taken to Lowellville and given a trial by Mayor Vogan, this morning. Both of them were convicted of adultery and sentenced to sixty days in the Cleveland work house. They were also assessed a fine of $150 and the costs. Attorney W. R. Graham, of this city, conducted the prosecution.

During the hearing it developed that the woman in the case had deserted one husband, married another, and at the time of her arrest was living with a third. Marsocci had also deserted a wife. The couple were arrested at the instance of the woman's second husband.

In Chapter 2 you were introduced to the term "grass widow", now here is a story of a "grass widower" ...

The New Castle News *(New Castle, PA) published on October 18, 1905:*

VALUABLE PROPERTY HERE INVOLVED IN LITIGATION

Joseph Fisher has filed a petition for divorce at Youngstown against his wife, alleging neglect, ill treatment and infidelity. He names Antonio Scopacasa as a co-respondent. He further alleges on account of such treatment on the part of his wife that he has been compelled to leave home and is now without means of support.

In his petition Fisher states that he was married to the defendant in 1879 and that they now have three children ranging in age from 12 to 22 years. He accuses his wife of gross neglect and that she has frequently assaulted him while they were living together and that she used vile and abusive language in the presence of their children.

According to the plaintiff's statement Mrs. Fisher now occupies the home in Lowellville together with the co-respondent Scopacasa, the two having lived there together since December 15, 1904. The property in Lowellville is valued at $3,000, and they also have property in New Castle, PA worth $5,000.

Historical Footnote: *Mr. Fisher was granted the divorce. His wife, Rosa Armando Fisher, then married Antonio Scopacasa and they remained together until her death in 1921.*

The Meehan Boiler Company of Lowellville was pressed into a nasty divorce case between one of its employees and his wife ...

The Youngstown Vindicator (Youngstown, OH) published February 2, 1908:

FEARS HUSBAND
Wife of Lowellville Mill Man Brings Suit for Divorce
Mrs. Loretta Kroll Alleges That Her Husband, Frank, Threatens to Take Her Life

Alleging that on last Sunday her husband, obtaining a revolver, assaulted and threatened to shoot her and take her life. Mrs. Loretta Kroll began suit for divorce through Attorney Frank Jacobs, Saturday. The defendant in the suit, Frank J. Kroll is foreman of the Meehan Boiler and Construction Co of Lowellville.

Mr. and Mrs. Kroll were married in Youngstown on January 28, 1902, just six years ago. The first act of violence that Mrs. Kroll complains of occurred in October, 1905, when she says he choked her, calling her vile names. This, she charges, he repeated in January, 1907, and at various times since. For than more than three years, she says he has been guilty of gross neglect and cruelty; that he has constantly assaulted and maltreated her. She adds that he is of a vicious, quarrelsome, and dangerous disposition. She believes that if he is allowed to live with her, he will do her bodily harm.

Mrs. Kroll sues for divorce and alimony and asks that the Meehan Construction company may be enjoined from paying her husband until the final determination of the case.

Historical Footnote: Frank was a German immigrant. The Kroll's divorce was granted and I was able to find Frank remarried sometime after 1910 and his second wife's name was Mary. Frank died on August 26, 1961 and it appears that his marriage to Mary was a long one. I was not able to find what happened to Loretta but I hope she found love again too.

Here is a funny story about an old man who should have known better...

The Youngstown Vindicator (Youngstown, OH) published on April 5, 1908:

VICTIM OF WOMEN'S WILES

Conrad Shaffer, Aged 70, Lost His Wallet Saturday Night - Blames Two Colored Girls

Conrad Shaffer, an old man from Lowellville, looking to be about 70 years old, visited West Commerce street Saturday night and fell a victim to the wiles of a pair of dusky belles. He lost his pocket-book.

Shaffer complained to Patrolman Sol Humphreys that the girls had enticed him into an alleyway and while pretending to caress him, extracted his wallet. The pocketbook contained no money, but held papers of value to the old Lothario. Patrolman Humphreys learned who the women were and their arrest was ordered.

Historical Footnote: Conrad was born in Prussia in 1841 and at the time of this incident had been a widower for four years, his wife was Sarah Cobb Shaffer. Before 1900 they had moved to Michigan, so it appears that Conrad was back in Ohio for a visit when this incident occurred. Conrad passed away on June 7, 1909, a little over a year after the incident.

One early summer night in 1913, our little village became the place where the lives of two young individuals, who had come to America to find a better life, were utterly destroyed.

The Youngstown Vindicator (Youngstown, OH) published on 3 June 1913:

TWO WOMEN SHOT DOWN BY AN INFURIATED LOVER

John Logar Fatally Injures His Intended Bride, Mary Sigmund, in Lowellville Monday Night and Painfully Wounds Mrs. Agnes Nogode – Was to Have Married the Girl Last Saturday – Tragedy Occurs in Home Where Girl Was Staying – Logar Was Arrested as He Tried to Escape – Eye Witness Tells of Shooting

"She fool me and I shoot her." said John Logar of Struthers as he sat with his head bowed in his hands this morning in the Lowellville jail after having shot his fiancée, Mary Sigmund, once in the neck and once in the back. The wounds will probably prove fatal. Mrs. Agnes Nogode, for whom Mary worked, was shot in the hip. Logar claims that he did not shoot Mrs. Nogode and probably did so unintentionally, as no reason for the act can be found and Logar apparently knows nothing of the third shot fired.

The shooting occurred last night about 9:15 o'clock in Lowellville in the kitchen of the Nogode saloon and lodging house. Jealousy is probably the motive for the act. The two victims were taken at once to the City hospital in Youngstown. The parties are Austrians.

According to the story of Marshal Tony Fisher of Lowellville and Mrs. Annie Drobnic, a sister of the girl victim of the tragedy who lives at the Nogode place, and who was the only uninjured witness of the shooting, Logar and Mary Sigmund were to have been married last Saturday. A lover's quarrel at the last moment caused a delay, which Logar apparently took as a permanent loss of affection.

That the girl is of a changeable disposition is evidenced by the fact that she told Marshal Tony Fisher on Saturday that she was through with Logar and that she would have nothing further to do with him. On Monday, she told Constable Roger Horn that she and Logar would want the house the first of the week which he had rented to them and was preparing for their occupancy.

Sister Tells Story

According to the story of Mrs. Annie Drobnic, the sister who witnessed the shooting, Mary and herself had been riding a merry-go-round, which is established on one of the side streets in Lowellville, early in the evening. Returning home about nine o'clock they found Logar there waiting for them. The girls entered by the back door into the kitchen and Logar came through from the barroom.

"Mary saw him and asked him to sit down," said Mrs. Drobnic. "I had my back turned and don't know whether he had the gun in his hand when he came into the room or not. The first I knew that trouble was coming was when he shot Mary through the neck. She started to run out the back door and he shot again, hitting her in the back. Just then Mrs. Nogode came running into the room and he shot at her. I don't know why, unless he was excited and thought she was going to try to stop his getting away. Logar ran back into the saloon and out into the street that way."

"Mrs. Nogode ran upstairs out onto the front porch and yelled to the neighbors for help. I don't remember much after that except seeing Mary lying there on the floor in a big pool of blood while blood squirted out on each side of her neck where the bullet went through."

Logar Ran Away

According to the story of Marshal Tony Fisher, William Hertz, police officer from Struthers, was visiting the police force in Lowellville. He and Officer Tom Driscoll happened to be in the immediate neighborhood when the shooting occurred. Hurrying to the scene they saw Logar running up the street. They ordered him to stop but he refused and ran faster. They fired one shot into the air as a warning, but were not called upon to make a target of the fugitive for the reason that his foot caught on some obstruction and he fell heavily. In his partially stunned condition there was no trouble taking him into custody.

When locked up Logar told Fisher that the girl had been "fooling him." He said that he had been calling on her for more than a year and she refused to marry him at the last moment. "I lose many days' work going to see her," said Logar. He is employed by the Youngstown Sheet and Tube company in the Struthers mill.

Bought Gun Saturday

"When did you buy the gun?" asked of Logar.
"I bought it last Saturday." he answered. He refused to tell from who the gun was purchased.
"Why did you shoot Mrs. Nogode?"
"I didn't shoot her." he said.
"How many shots did you fire?"
"Two." Was the answer. He seemed to have no knowledge of firing the third shot at Mrs. Nogode.

Pools of Blood

Clothing, floors and stairs were marked with blood stains where pools of blood from the wounded woman had coagulated and dried. At one point where Mrs. Nogode stood on the front upper porch and cried for help, a pool of half-dried blood still remained this morning. The two victims must have bled profusely before they were removed.

Hearing Today

Mayor John Roller of Lowellville stated that Logar's hearing will probably be held this afternoon. He is waiting for some word from hospital officials as whether the girl will live or die. Roller said "he will be bound over to the grand jury for indictment."

Historical Footnote: *Agnes recovered but Mary's conditioned worsened. Peritonitis set in and there was no medical miracle that could save the 22 year-old's life. Her parents brought her to their home near Robinson Township, PA to die. Mary succumbed to her injuries on June 18th, after having lingered for over two weeks after John Logar shot her.*

Logar was charged with first degree murder and held for trial. At his trial in November 1913, John Logar pleaded guilty to a lesser charge of second degree murder and was sentenced to life in prison. He was twenty-six years old. The last record that I was able to find for John Logar is the 1920 census where he is listed as an inmate at the Ohio Penitentiary in Columbus. Since he received a sentence of life in prison, it can be presumed that he died in prison and is buried somewhere in Ohio in a potter's field. Mary is buried in Petrie Cemetery near her family's home in Robinson Township.

4 HORRIFIC ACCIDENTS

With the mills, quarries and railroad tracks located in and around Lowellville, there were, over the years, a number of horrific accidents. In reading these articles, I was often amazed how the newspapers of the time reported such graphic details about the accidents and injuries sustained by the victims. Sadly, most of the time, due to a lack of the advanced medical care available today, these unfortunates had little chance for survival.

One of the earliest articles I found was a short article about three drowning deaths on the Pennsylvania-Ohio Canal. The canal ran along the Mahoning River through the village. In fact our present day Water Street was once called Canal Street due to its proximity to the canal and tow path.

The Daily Cleveland Herald *(Cleveland, OH) published on April 25, 1856.*

DROWNED

We learn that three Welshmen named Thos. Brown, Richard Brown, and William Humphrey, were drowned in the Canal, at Lowellville, on Tuesday night of last week. It was the night of the severe storm, and they were making their way to the village upon the tow-path, but whether they were blown into the Canal, or got in some other way, is not known. They all leave wives and young children.

Historical Footnote: *The canal was 82 miles long, had 54 locks and connected New Castle, Pennsylvania to Akron, Ohio. It took five years to build at a cost of over $1.2M and was completed in 1840. When the railroads came into the area, the business on the canal diminished and it was abandoned by 1872. Today there is no visible trace of the canal in the village.*

I found these two brief stories on the same day in the same paper and thought that it was quite a sad coincidence that such similar accidents happened at the same time in Lowellville and nearby Struthers ...

The Pittsburg Dispatch *(Pittsburg, PA) published on March 17, 1892:*

William Grist's two little children at Lowellville, near Youngstown, were scalded to death yesterday morning. They had upset a kettle of boiling water from a stove.

Two children of Mrs. Thomas Price, of Struthers, O., upset a boiler of hot water yesterday and were scalded to death. The mother is prostrate with grief.

Here is a story that highlights just how difficult it could be to discover the identity of a deceased individual in an era when folks often traveled from town to town looking for work. When I read stories like this one I always find myself wondering if there was a family in Europe who spent the rest of their lives wondering what had happened to their loved one.

The Youngstown Vindicator *(Youngstown, OH) published on August 2, 1892:*

UNKNOWN MAN
Mangled and Killed by a Train Today
Steps from one track to Death That followed on in Another – The Deceased Had Money and Tailor's Tools

An unknown man was instantly killed this morning about 7 o'clock by a local P. & L. E. freight train 44, between Struthers and Lowellville.

The man was walking on the track when he was run down. Where the accident happened, the road is double tracked and the man was walking towards this city on the right hand side in the middle of the track. A train was approaching him from behind and he deliberately stepped off the track on to the other and directly in front of the freight engine pulling train 44, and which was going south at a lively rate at the time. The unfortunate fellow was caught by the cow catcher and his brains dashed out against the pilot of the engine, which threw his body on top of a high embankment to the right of the road. The train was stopped, but before the train hands could get to him, the man was dead. He never knew what killed him.

His skull was crushed in over the right eye and both legs were broken, one below the knee and the other at the left ankle.

Coroner Welsh was called, and after reviewing the remains he ordered them brought to this city. They were placed on the next passenger train and removed to the morgue of Drake & Pitts, where the body will be prepared for burial awaiting word from relatives or friends, if it is possible to find them.

The dead man is a German, and from the tools he carried with him he was evidently a tailor. He had a pair of tailor's shears, needles and thread and a thimble. In a bundle tied up in paper he carried some dirty shirts and underclothing. In his pocket was found a receipt for board issued to Peter Moner from a hotel keeper named Schweitzer, at Cumberland, Md. It is possible that this is his name, and word will be sent to that city in quest of information in regard to him.

In a canvas envelope, similar to a tobacco pouch, was found $19 in money. This envelope pouch bore the printed advertisement of the Merchants and Traders Bank of Brunswick, Georgia. The description of the man as given by the coroner is as follows: Height five feet, one inch; weight, 130; age, about 30 years; dark hair, brown eyes, small brown mustache, round face and well developed body. The poor unfortunate had on clean clothes and his body showed that it was well cared for. He had on a brand new pair of pants, the buttons of which bore the name of a tailor named Aland of Butler, PA.

The body will be held here the required time, awaiting word from relatives.

The following article is a follow-up to the article above. In the first article the victim's possible name was published as Peter Moner, but in this article the name is Peter Mouer. It appears that the man was buried in a Youngstown area potter's field, as no one claimed his remains.

The Youngstown Evening Vindicator *(Youngstown, OH) published on August 3, 1892:*

STILL UNSOLVED
The Identity of the Man Killed on the Tracks Yesterday

The identity of the German who was killed by the cars at Lowellville yesterday, is still unsolved. The local Tailors' Union telegraphed to New York last night to find out if the deceased is a member of the Tailors' Union in good standing, and if they receive word that he is, the funeral will be held at the expense of the Tailor's Union.

The name sent on was the same as given on the receipt for board, found in the dead man's pocket.

The remains have been prepared for internment and will be buried tomorrow morning at 10 o'clock, if no word is received.

Coroner Welsh is of the opinion that the man is a tramp. He thinks that the name, Peter Mouer, given on the board receipt, is the name of the deceased. The fact that the man had money, and tools does not indicate, however, that the deceased was a tramp.

The coroner has ordered that the body be interred for sanitary reasons on account of decomposition due to the terrible injuries which caused death.

I bet poor Mrs. Moore had quite a headache ... but she was lucky to have survived...

The Salem Daily News *(Salem, OH) published on February 3, 1897:*

DRAGGED BY RUNAWAY HORSE

Mrs. H. A. Moore of Lowellville was driving into the city yesterday when her horse ran away. She pluckily held to the lines after she was thrown out until she was dragged against a stone pile, tearing her scalp in a horrible manner. Surgeons placed 30 stitches in the wounds, after which she was taken home.

The Youngstown Vindicator *(Youngstown, OH) published on December 4, 1897:*

INSTANT DEATH
Mike Smith, a Laborer at the Lowellville Furnace, Met It

Yesterday
His Neck was Broken
A Mistaken Signal the Cause of the Most Horrible Accident

A frightful and sudden death was the lot of Mike Smith or Krispinsky, a Slav, employed at the furnace of the Ohio Iron and Steel Co., at Lowellville, Friday afternoon.

Smith was employed at the hoisting cage and was known as a "bottom filler". He was at the time when death overtook him, engaged in putting in a couple of barrows on the cage that was down, and had the second barrow partly on when the "top filler" started the cage. The cages move rapidly and Smith had not time to move; he was caught between the iron girders and the cage and squeezed, carried up a distance and finally fell off. His death must have been instantaneous as his skull was badly broken, as well as his neck.

The cages are moved up and down by bell signal and the "top filler" who started the cage says that the dead man rung the bell for him. Whether this is true or not will never be known, but certain it is that the accident resulted from the "top filler" believing he heard the bell.

The accident was of such a sudden and distressing character and coming under such peculiar conditions, that it has called forth the sympathy of the entire people for the dead man's family. He leaves a young widow and a baby child. Smith, like most of his race employed about the furnaces, knew only to work and sleep, yet he was devoted to his young wife, was thrifty and sober and well regarded by those who knew him.

Historical Footnote: His widow having no means of support as result of the death of her husband, filed a lawsuit for wrongful death against the mill for $10,000 in 1898. There were few options left for a woman in her situation as there were no death benefits from either an employer or the federal government like those which are available today.

The New Castle News (New Castle, PA) published on March 9, 1898:

MET INSTANT DEATH
Alva McMahon Ground to a Pulp at a Grade Crossing

Alva McMahon, a teamster, was instantly killed late Monday afternoon in a grade crossing accident at Lowellville. The unfortunate man's body was fairly ground to a pulp under the wheels of a Pittsburgh, Youngstown and Ashtabula freight engine. McMahon was a teamster in the employ of a Mr. Baker of Struthers. He was driving a two-horse wagon into Lowellville, and had just crossed the P. Y. & A track when his horses took fright at an engine standing on the switch, turning suddenly and overturned the wagon on the tracks. The vehicle was overturned on the main line directly in front of the freight approaching from the West. McMahon fell underneath the wagon and was plowed down. Although the air brakes were promptly applied to the train and the engine reversed, it was impossible to stop it until the damage was done. McMahon was killed instantly. Both horses broke loose from the wagon and were uninjured. McMahon was a young man and lived with Mr. Baker at Struthers. He had friends in the seventh ward, where he was well known.

This is a tragic story of a young man finding his older brother's body on the train tracks. The accident occurred in the winter when trains where likely to be transporting coal. It was not unusual for villagers to "borrow" coal from passing freight trains ... Charles, the victim, was known to do this and it may have been the reason for his proximity to the train.

The New Castle News *(New Castle, PA) published on January 27, 1901:*

KILLED BY THE CARS
A YOUNG MAN, CHARLES E. ALLSHOUSE OF NEAR LOWELLVILLE

CUT IN TWO BY A FREIGHT TRAIN YESTERDAY AFTERNOON - MANAGLED BODY FOUND BY HIS BROTHER

Charles E. Allshouse, who lived with his parents about a mile east of Lowellville, was killed yesterday evening between 3 and 4 o'clock on the Pennsylvania Road.

Allshouse, who was about twenty years of age, at the time indicated, ran hatless out of the house and attempted to board a passing freight train that was running west. Shortly after the train passed the house, which is twenty-five or thirty feet back from the railroad, a brother of the victim went out and found the body on the track. The body had been cut squarely in two at the hips and the left arm had been severed. No one saw the accident, and the boy, aged thirteen was the first to discover the remains.

A man of Lowellville happened along and notified the agent at that place. He sent word to Undertaker Cunningham also of Lowellville, and he went to the scene of the accident and removed the remains to the home of the parents. Word was sent here to Coroner R. M. Morrison. He went down on the street car and made an investigation, finding the facts as stated. He returned last night about 11:30 and has decided that no inquest is necessary.

The coroner was informed by relatives of the deceased that he had been warned not to board passing trains. He had now and then jumped on cars and tumbled off some coal, so his brother said last night. It is not likely that the young man had intended to take an extended trip when it is a fact that he ran out of the house and to the train without his hat.

Historical footnote: The younger brother who discovered the body was most likely Albert, who had just turned 13 years old in December of 1900. They were the children of James and Laura (Shindledecker) Allhouse. Charles was born in April of 1881. He was the oldest of six children - Hugh born in 1883, Anna born in 1885, Albert born in 1887, Ella born in 1890 and Hildah born in 1897. Albert named one of his sons Charles, I assume it was after the brother he lost.

Time and time again when reading stories like one the below, it just continues to surprise me how dangerous the working conditions were in the late eighteenth and early nineteenth centuries. What's especially sad about this case is that the victim left behind a disabled widow who had no surviving family to care for her.

The Youngstown Vindicator *(Youngstown, OH) published on January 16, 1909:*

CUT IN TWO
Charles Mitchell of Lowellville Meets Terrible Death at Carbon Engine Run Off the Dump
Pathetic Incident Connected With the Accident of Saturday

Charles Mitchell, a resident of Lowellville, 50 years of age, met instant death at the Carbon limestone works near here Saturday morning at 11:30. He was in charge of one of the dinkey engines at the plant when it run over the "dump" cutting his body in two. The engine backed one of the cars too near the edge of the "stripping bank" and in a second, the car and locomotive were over the dump. The supposition is that Mr. Mitchell was thrown under the engine.

The deceased had lived in Lowellville for years and years and among the people of the town, as well as associates at Carbon, was held in the very highest esteem. Physically, he was a very powerful man and was known for his genial ways and kindness of the heart. His devotion to his wife, who is not well, was admired generally. The task of communicating the sad news to her was one of the pathetic things in connection with the accident. The first messenger told of an accident in which he was slightly hurt, a later one gradually revealing the true condition of affairs. All of their children are dead, the last daughter having passed away two years ago.

No thought has as yet been given to arrangements for the funeral, the body being still at Cunningham's morgue.

This is such a heartbreaking story, the main reason I included it is because since this little one died over a century ago she is most likely forgotten. There is saying that no one truly dies as long as there is someone left on earth to speak their name. So when you read this story, speak little Grace's name.

The Youngstown Vindicator *(Youngstown, OH) published on August 18, 1909:*

LITTLE GIRL KILLED BY STREET CAR

Grace Marie Miles Run Down While Playing Along the Track Near Lowellville Tuesday - Motorman Did Not See the Victim - Traveling Man Witnessed the Accident

Her golden curls matted with blood and her little body terribly crushed, Grace Marie Miles, six years old, was found lying beside the Mahoning Valley tracks near Stop 24, west of Lowellville, Tuesday afternoon about 3 o'clock. Her skull was fractured and the left arm was broken in several places. Death was instantaneous.

The exact manner in which the child met her death is not known, but it is thought that she was struck by car No. 143 in charge of Motorman Dickson and Conductor Phelps. When found the body was between the Mahoning Valley and the B. & O. tracks. A traveling man, whose name could not be learned, declared, after the body was discovered, that he saw the car strike the child. Motorman Dickinson declares that he did not see the child on the track, nor did he know that he had run her down. The traction company officials admit however that the child might have come out of the weeds near the track and been struck by the step on the blind side of the car.

The traveling man who claims he saw the car run down the little girl, declares he heard Motorman Dickinson blow his whistle when about 100 yards from where the little girl was killed. Upon the return trip to the city this way several people tried to flag the car to inform the motorman of the accident, but declare that he refused to stop.

Coroner C. M. Klyne investigated the death and the circumstances surrounding the sad case and declared that the child was run down by car No. 143. He rendered a verdict of death due to a fractured skull as the result of being struck by a traction car.

The mangled body was carried to the Whetstone home nearby. The mother of the child was away and did not know that the little one had been killed until she returned.

The funeral will be held from the family home near Lowellville Thursday afternoon at 2 o'clock with internment in the Lowellville cemetery.

Historical Footnote: Grace was born on May 19, 1903 in Pennsylvania. Her parents were Samuel and Myrtle (Whetstone) Miles. In the 1910 Census Myrtle is shown as being divorced and living with her parents the Whetstones. It does not appear she had any other children when Grace died.

After I found this story, I had to find out if the victim, Mr. Perry, survived. He seemed to be a real scrapper and if anyone could survive being run over by a train, it could have been him!

The Olympia Daily Recorder *(Olympia, WA) published on October 22, 1910:*

CRAWLS QUARTER MILE CARRYING SEVERED LEGS

A freight crew which responded to a frantic signal for assistance from a man on the Baltimore and Ohio railroad track near Lowellville, found Thomas Perry of Lincoln, Neb., sitting with a leg in each hand. His legs had been cut off below his knees.

"Say give me a cigarette boys while I am telling you about it. I have been here for ages without a smoke," said Perry. "I was stealing a ride and fell off. When the train went by I picked up my legs and started to crawl. It was very dark and I finally found I could not go any further. Then I began to pray for the light."

The trip to Youngstown was 15 minutes, during which Perry smoked cigarettes and drank coffee. He was conscious when taken to the city hospital and is still alive. Perry had lain for six hours alongside the track after dragging himself for nearly a quarter of a mile.

Historical Footnote: Thomas Perry did not survive the accident, he died on October 15, 1910 in Youngstown, Ohio.

In my research I came across several articles about John Igo and his son who shared his name. Neither of them seemed to be model citizens and it makes one wonder if the younger John would have turned out better if he had a different father.

The New Castle News (New Castle, PA) published on March 21, 1911:

LOWELLVILLE YOUTH SHOOTS GRANDFATHER

To save his aged grandmother from abuse and to protect himself, Noble Shrodes, 18 years old, shot and seriously wounded his grandfather, John Igo, aged 64 years, at the home in Lowellville Sunday evening. Igo was taken to city hospital suffering from bullet wounds in both legs. He is alleged to have gone home Sunday night in an ugly humor and abused his wife. The grandson interfered and Igo tried to assault him. Young Shrodes secured a revolver and warned his grandfather to keep back. The old man tried to get hold of him and the boy fired twice, both bullets taking effect, one in each of his legs. Shrodes was arrested but was released on his own recognizance.

Historical Footnote: John Igo survived the shooting but only to die four years later in a train accident. The article describing his death follows below.

The New Castle News *(New Castle, PA) published on September 20, 1915:*

OLD MAN KILLED AT LOWELLVILLE
John Igo, Resident of Village for 50 Years, Struck by P. & L. E. Train

Westbound passenger train number 23, on the P & L. E., struck and instantly killed John Igo, a venerable resident of Lowellville at the Fifth Street crossing at 5:10 p.m. Saturday. The body was taken to Orr's morgue in Youngstown.

Mr. Igo was 75 years of age. No one seems to have seen the aged man killed, but it is supposed that he started across the track and did not notice the approach of the fast train. His body was badly mangled. The train was stopped and the remains were taken aboard the train to Youngstown where they were met and carried to the morgue in Orr's ambulance.

Mr. Igo, it is said, had resided in Lowellville for fifty or more years. His wife died three years ago. One daughter survives.

The Pennsylvania and Ohio Electric Light Company Power Plant was built between 1912 and 1913. At the time it opened, it was the most modern power plant in the world and considered a marvel of technology. Hundreds of men were recruited from around the country to work for the plant contractor, Stone & Webster. It was located east of town, its tall stacks can often be seen in vintage village photos that face east. It was decommissioned in the 1950s and replaced with the current Ohio Edison Substation that is just outside the village limits and viewable from the Stavich Bike Trail. In this article we learn about the death of one of the workers hired by Stone & Webster.

The Youngstown Vindicator *(Youngstown, OH) published on December 17, 1912:*

FATAL SHOCK
Employee of Stone & Webster Killed at Lowellville Power Station

C. A. Bailey, a resident of Sandy Lake, Mercer County PA., and a machinist in the employ of Stone and Webster, contractors working on the new powerhouse east of Lowellville, was instantly killed Tuesday forenoon when his hand accidentally came in contact with a wire carrying 22,000 volts of electricity.

At the time of the accident Bailey was up on a scaffold assisting the adjustment of some electrical machinery. Suddenly he stepped backward and laid his hand on what is known as a copper bus, which is a wire connected with outside wire and carries electricity to the transmitter. As his hand came in contact with the wire, his body stiffened with shock. The man did not fall but the body remained fast to the wire, until it was removed by fellow workmen. Several physicians were summoned and exerted every effort to resuscitate the man. Life could not be brought back, however, and after it had been viewed by Coroner Cross, the body was taken to Cunningham's morgue in Lowellville where it will be prepared for burial.

C. A. Bailey was a resident of Sandy Lake but had been boarding in New Castle since he has been working in Lowellville.

Historical Footnote: *Mr. Bailey was born in 1870 and was 42 years old when he died. He is buried in Sandy Lake, PA.*

Less than three months later another death occurred at the power plant shortly after it went into operation… this death was caused by the big flood of 1913.

On Easter Sunday, March 23, 1913 rain began falling across the Midwest and after three days of heavy rain, flooding occurred, with Ohio and Indiana being particularly hard hit. By the time the flood waters dissipated, over 650 people were dead making this flood at the time the second most deadliest flood in America (behind the 1899 flood in Johnstown, PA when over 2,200 people were killed). All of the communities in the Mahoning Valley along the river were impacted and Lowellville had one drowning death. Here is the report on the death of James Dunn, who died trying to help his fellow co-workers. James was an Austrian immigrant and is buried somewhere in Lowellville cemetery:

The Youngstown Vindicator *(Youngstown, OH) published on March 26, 1913:*

LOSES LIFE
Hero on Way for Help Perishes at Lowellville Wednesday

James Dunn, aged 23 years, was drowned in the Mahoning river at 9:30 am Wednesday. He lost his life while attempting to make his way across the water from the new Mahoning Valley power house which is entirely surrounded. His body was swept away in the flood. Dunn's home is in Pittsburgh, but he roomed in Youngstown.

Dunn, who was the night fireman at the power plant, with fourteen other men, had been imprisoned in the works without food. Wednesday morning friends from the shore threw out a rope to them long enough to reach from the land to the plant. A rude raft was fashioned on which Dunn and a companion, Samuel Eaton, attempted to get over to the town to procure food for the rest of the men.

When half way across the rude craft turned over, throwing both men into the water. Eaton grabbed the raft and made a heroic attempt to rescue Dunn, but because of the frantic struggles of the drowning man, was unable to save him.

Here is a story about what could have been a tragedy, but this young lady got lucky and survived her injuries, lived to adulthood, married and had two children ...

The Youngstown Vindicator *(Youngstown, OH) published on November 2, 1914:*

GIRL SHOT IN THE HEAD
**Penelope Houston of Lowellville Victim of Accidental Shooting
At Play When Rifle Is Discharged
Bullet Makes Two Ugly Wounds, One in the Temple and Other
Over Right Eye**

Miss Penelope Houston had a narrow escape from being instantly killed Saturday evening when she was accidentally shot in the head. Miss Houston had gone to the home of a neighbor to spend the evening with several other young people, they went out to play hide and seek. One of the boys had a rifle with him and it accidentally went off, the bullet making two ugly wounds, one in the temple and the other over the right eye. If the bullet had struck Miss Houston one-eighth of an inch lower it would have caused instant death. The young man who had the rifle is almost frantic with grief. A doctor was summoned immediately and gave the necessary medical aid. She is resting as well as could be expected, but cannot tell what the outcome will be for several days yet.

Historical Footnote: *Penelope was born on June 4, 1900 in Pennsylvania to Samuel S. Houston and Lucia Hayworth Houston. She grew up in Lowellville and lived with her aunts Miss Margaret Houston and Mrs. Ruth Houston Yeo. She eventually married Earl E. Parks and they lived near Nashville, TN. She and Earl had two children - Hayworth Parks and Margaret (Betty) Parks Humphrey. Despite her luck as a young girl, Penelope did not live a long life, she died at the age of 34 of a heart ailment on March 10, 1935. Her death was unexpected.*

This accident may not have been very tragic but does show that even hundred years ago there were impatient drivers!

The Youngstown Vindicator *(Youngstown, OH) published on July 13, 1917:*

Miss Eve Houston was painfully though not seriously injured Wednesday when her horse ran away on the cemetery hill, throwing her out of the buggy and dragging her some distance. She received a large cut across the forehead, several cuts on her cheek and her shoulder and back was badly bruised. Ms. Houston was returning from town and was passing another buggy on the hill when an automobile driven by Mr. Burns tried to pass between the two buggies and caught Miss Houston's buggy completely wrecking it and causing the horse to run away.

Historical footnote: *Eve Houston was born on June 9, 1858 on the Houston Farm. She died on October 15, 1921 and is buried in the Lowellville cemetery.*

In her obituary she was described "as a woman of high character, beloved by all in the community and held in high regard as an authority of many important topics of genuine interest to the community in which she always took a keen interest."

5 DISASTEROUS FIRES

Fires in Lowellville often led to disastrous results due to the fact that most homes and businesses were constructed of wood materials and were located close to one another. Even though the village did eventually organize a fire department, its early equipment was primitive and at times firefighters had to resort to stopping large conflagrations by use of dynamite!

Compounding the risk, fire insurance was very expensive and many home and business owners were either underinsured or not insured at all — causing families to suffer great financial loss due to fires. The most notable fire was the fire of February 1917 when four blocks of town were essentially wiped out. Much of the area consumed by this fire, to this day, still does not have many buildings on it.

In most of the reports of fires, miraculously there were few instances of loss of life, but property damage was high. Lowellville knew it needed a fire department and struggled for years to establish one, in this 1901 article it seemed like the prospects were good but it would actually take another six years for the fire department to be formally established ...

The New Castle News *(New Castle, PA) published on January 19, 1901:*

LOWELLVILLE LATEST
It Will Endeavor to Secure a Fire Department

The village of Lowellville is about to take another step farther in the way of progress and advancement.

Attorney L. H. E. Lowry said Saturday that on January 24th the voters of the village would hold a special election and vote on the question of issuing bonds for the purpose of establishing a fire department.

At present the village has no fire protection whatever and the town would be at the mercy of the flames in the event of a big conflagration. It is proposed to issue bonds in the sum of $1,000. If the bond issue meets the approval of the voters, the village will buy a fire engine and establish a fire department that will be of some service at least in the event of a big fire. The fire department would be a volunteer affair and no one would be paid for their services in fighting the flames when they would put in an appearance. There is a good prospect of the bond issue receiving the necessary vote to insure the establishment of a department and if it does, no time is to be lost in buying the necessary apparatus.

The village was bonded some time ago in the sum of $8,000 to establish an electric light plant and no one seems sorry for it, and all who have been heard to express themselves on the fire department question seem to be in favor of it.

Six months after the article above, Lowellville's bucket brigade was able to save the village from another fire disaster. The first article tells of a rumor reporting that Lowellville was totally engulfed in flames and would be wiped off the map. The second one is actually an account from the mayor of Lowellville, Porter Watson, on the fire which involved only one house, the old Watson homestead.

The Youngstown Vindicator *(Youngstown, Ohio) both published on May 6, 1901.*

FALSE REPORT

Currently rumored yesterday that Lowellville was afire. Many Youngstown People Attracted to the Scene Were Agreeably Disappointed

A report reached the city yesterday that the entire village of Lowellville was in flames and was in danger of destruction. It was currently reported that Lowellville would soon be wiped off the face of the earth by one of the worst fires that ever visited Mahoning county. Just as soon as the rumor reached this city, a number of local people jumped on the street cars and made a hasty trip to the little village to see what was really the matter. Upon their arrival in Lowellville the town looked to be in its natural condition and there was not even a sign of a fire, a fact which agreeably disappointed the Youngstown delegation attracted there by the sensational reports in circulation.

It appears that a roof of a house was on fire early in the afternoon, and the impression immediately got out that the whole town was in flames.

Among the first to get to Lowellville after they heard the report were R. Montgomery, John P. Hazlett, John Beil and they stood ready to fight the fire demon in the event their services being necessary.

Below is a letter to the **Vindicator** *Editor from Lowellville mayor, Porter Watson, who gave a detailed account of the men who helped save the village from disaster. The home that had caught fire was built by his father, William Watson, who had settled in Lowellville in the 1830s.*

FIRE IN LOWELLVILLE
Gallant Work of the Citizens With Bucket Brigade
Editor Vindicator

On Sunday about 11 o'clock a.m., Charles McMillen discovered the old Watson homestead to be on fire. He let out a few yells of "Fire! Fire!" and in a very short space of time everybody was running with buckets in hand, but before they were perfectly organized and succeeded in reaching the roof of the building, the whole structure was in flames and all hopes of saving the building seemed hopeless. A line of buckets was instantly formed and a perfect flood of water was poured into the building for an hour when it was gotten under control and the fire finally extinguished. It was the best battle against fire with a bucket brigade ever seen by anybody. There were heroes by the dozen, all of whom done themselves proud, and but for their timely assistance, the whole of the front of Main street would have been in ruins.

Messrs. Collins, Bake, McBride, Meehans, Nock, Davidon, Schontz, Wymer, Dahringher and a score of others worked as they never worked before to extinguish the flames. The Italians, men and women, formed in the line and seemed to me as if they were working for their lives to assist in putting out the fire. Mr. McNeven, who lived in the house, had everything carried out and his furniture and everything was badly damaged and he has the sympathy of the entire community.

Great credit is given to W. S. McCombs , of the furnace company, for his kindly sending over every man that could be spared from the works to assist us at the fire. I wish to express my heartfelt thanks through the **Vindicator**, to one and all for the gallant work they done in savings what they did of one of the oldest landmarks in Lowellville.

(signed) PORTER WATSON

Even though a fire department was eventually established, it still struggled to contain large fires such as this one in 1911 on the South Side that caused much damage. It was lack of city water mains in the village that kept the fire department from being able to control the fire at its origin. While attempting to put the fire out, the fire department found that its hose was too short to reach the river, its water source, and it had to rely on a stream that ran near the Sharon Steel mill. This limitation, enabled the fire to spread rapidly.

The Plain Dealer *(Cleveland, OH) published on June 7, 1911:*

FLEE WITH BABES AS VILLAGE BURNS

Screaming Mothers Throng Streets of Lowellville as Midnight Fire Rages
Their Homes Aflame, Citizens Find Blaze Resistant

The entire south section of Lowellville, a town of 2,000 people, seven miles east of here on the Mahoning river, is threatened with destruction by fire which started at 11:30 tonight, and aid is being dispatched from Youngstown.

At midnight, the flames has consumed eight houses and the big general store of J. A. Lomax. The fire is spreading both ways along the river, and it is believed that few buildings in the residence and commercial sections will escape.

Lowellville is situated on both sides of the river, the south section being largely devoted to the homes of employees of the Ohio Iron & Steel Co.'s blast furnaces. Many of the residents are foreigners, and a panic is ruling the community. Mothers are rushing about with babies in their arms, screaming and hysterical, and in several cases women have had to be restrained by force from rushing back into blazing dwellings to save some prized article or forgotten hoard, accumulated by laborious toil.

Fire Starts in Saloon

The fire started in the saloon of Joseph Ferraro, on the main street, and spread with great rapidity. The buildings are all of frame construction and stand close together. One house no sooner is blazing than those on either side first begin to smoke and within a few minutes are wrapped as in a seething furnace.

The town practically has no fire protection and bucket brigades are helpless to check spread of the flames. Men are standing around dazed by the misfortune which has overtaken them and offer no aid to those who are still trying to stem the fiery tide. There is little wind, but what there is, is fitful and only aids in fanning the blaze as it spreads east and west along the river.

Apparatus from here is being rushed to Lowellville on flat cars, and with the river to draw from, the steamers may be able to save a portion of the town, if they arrive in time.

The north section of the town, on the other bank of the Mahoning, contains a better class of residents and stores and is not threatened.

Here is the second article about the 1911 fire…

The Marion Daily Star *(Marion, OH) published on June 7, 1911 and also in* **The Marion Weekly Star** *published on June 10, 1911:*

DISASTEROUS FIRE HITS LOWELLVILLE

Fire and dynamite razed an entire square here today, while more than thirty families watched the destruction of their homes. When the fire broke out in V. Di Oto's saloon, on Washington Street, at an hour before midnight, the whole square was aroused. Within ten minutes, the flames had leaped across the street before a west wind and had communicated it to the first home.

The village fire department was handicapped with inadequate equipment and the village authorities resorted to dynamite to halt the fire. They blew up four houses.

One detachment of firemen led by ex-mayor Varley, was in back of a house, unaware that a charge of dynamite had been put under it. When the blast came, the debris was blown on them, but they escaped serious injury.

An appeal to the Youngstown Fire Department brought apparatus and firemen on a special train and the fire was finally controlled. The loss is $75,000.

Historical Footnote: *The aftermath was quite a spectacle and it was later reported in the newspaper that over 10,000 people came to the village via street car and* *automobiles to view the ruins.*

Just six year later, the worst fire to ever impact Lowellville occurred in the early morning hours of February 19, 1917. Here are two very detailed articles about the devastation of the 1917 fire. Over a hundred years later, you can still see its impact in the open space that exists within the areas bounded by Wood, First, Third, and Liberty Streets.

The Youngstown Vindicator *(Youngstown, OH) published on February 20, 1917:*

LOWELLVILLE FIRE RUMORS
Many Stories Circulated Relative to Starting of Monday's Blaze
Reports circulated freely in Lowellville Tuesday relative to the conflagration Monday morning intimate that the robbing of the safe at Kiefer & Co. liquor store may have been done by local talent. The police state that the old safe has been in Lowellville long enough for scores of people to learn the combination.

It is agreed that the fire was of incendiary origin. So suspicious is the whole affair that the state fire marshal's office may detail a man to Lowellville to make a thorough investigation, citizens say. Rumors are rife and many assert that they can see a motive for the wiping out of the old block. It is possible, however, that the true cause of the fire may never be known.

At a meeting of the village council held Monday night, a committee consisting of James Woods, Andrew Spohrer and Henry Schrader was authorized to investigate the merits of a triplex pump, hose and chemical wagon made with a Ford chassis by the Howe Manufacturing company and equipped to carry 150 feet of chemical hose, 800 feet of ordinary hose, besides having other advantages. This committee may decide also to see other fire apparatus of this same type demonstrated. A new truck is to be purchased at once, according council's action.

With modern firefighting apparatus in the service of the village Monday morning it is believed that the blaze would not have spread from the building where it originated. The old hand pump attached to the antiquated fire engine, failed to make any impression on the conflagration. The water had to be carried a distance of 500 feet from the river. The pressure was weak and the stream entirely too small. Without hydrants, the fire apparatus from Youngstown could render little service.

Engineer's Statement

William Wilson, of this city, engineer of Lowellville village, stated Tuesday that if the new fire system had been in use, the blaze would have been kept where it originated. He expects to see the water works in operation by next August. Just as soon as the cold weather is over construction work will be resumed again in earnest. When the water mains are in and the system working, insurance rates will be lowered in the village, it is predicted.

High insurance rates have proven a burden to Lowellville property owners for years.

Rev. Robert Humphreys, pastor of the Presbyterian church, which was destroyed by the fire, announces a meeting of the church trustees for tonight, to decide where to hold services next Sunday. The Presbyterian church was a landmark in Lowellville, having been erected 63 years ago. During all of that time, the Lowery, Moore and Robinson families have been attending services there. Lowellville at the time the church was built was a struggling village, gaining prominence because of its advantageous location on the Cleveland and Pittsburgh canal. The congregation carried $3,500 fire insurance on the church building and $700 on the furnishings, making a total of $4,200.

The M. E. congregation carried $3,300 fire insurance on its edifice. The church was also totally destroyed. C. W. Danforth, district superintendent for the M. E. church in this district, plans to hold a conference with the trustees of the church and devise ways and means for rebuilding the edifice. Both churches are likely to be rebuilt on the old sites.

This is the second article in **The Youngstown Vindicator** *(Youngstown, OH) published on February 19, 1917:*

BIG FIRE AT LOWELLVILLE MAY BE ROBBERS' WORK
Entire Square in Village Wiped Out and Cracksmen Are Suspected – Loss Will Amount to More than $60,000
Fifteen Horses Lose Their Lives, Two Churches, Two Livery Barns, Stores and Residences Destroyed in Early Morning Conflagration
Dynamite Check Progress of Flames

Fire, the origin of which is not yet determined, and which was discovered about 3:20 a.m. Monday, practically wiped out the square of frame buildings bounded by Second, Third, Liberty and Wood Streets in Lowellville, destroying two churches, and more than a dozen business establishments and dwellings. A total estimated loss on buildings of more than $60,000 and a loss on contents of business houses coupled with the death of 15 horses which perished in the flames, adds $10,000 more. The Lowellville Fire Department, which consists of one hand-operated horse cart and one hand chemical apparatus, was unable to cope with the blaze and fire engines sent from Youngstown in response to a call for aid, were unable to raise water from the river.

The theory regarding the origin of the fire given most credence by residents of the village, is that it was kindled by burglars who are believed to have robbed the safe of Kiefer & Co.'s liquor store Sunday night. T. F. Varley and Eugene Braatz entered the store shortly after the fire was discovered, and found $522 missing from the safe and checks and other papers scattered all over the floor. The safe was closed and locked but the condition of the lock indicated that it had been tampered with. No indication of how the thieves gained entrance could be found as the rear of the store was in flames when the robbery was discovered.

Other Theories Advanced

Other theories are that the fire started in a building owned by Dan Steiner of this city and occupied by a stable by Joe Melillo and another that it may have started in a pool room, run by J. E. Giles. All of these business places were in adjoining buildings, J. E. Giles who resided over his pool room, gave the first alarm of the fire to members of the village police department who were in the city hall at the time. Flames and smoke were issuing from the building in which the pool room is located when the firemen reached the scene.

The heaviest losers by fire were Carl E. Braatz, who owned the property on Liberty street occupied by Sam DeSalvo's warehouse, Kiefer & Co.'s liquor store and saloon; W. Collins' barber shop, and Sam DeSalvo's grocery and dwelling; as well as that occupied by J. S. McConnell's livery barn on Third Street; Nick Catone, who owned the double dwelling house at Second and Liberty Street, occupied by George Cluse and J. Barnhardt, the residence of George Thorpe of Liberty Street, the Herbert Flattery residence and his own residence on Second Street and Dan Steiner of this city, who owned the property in Liberty Street occupied by Mrs. Louis Freeman's restaurant; J. E. Giles' barber shop; Harry Hall's pool room and bowling alley, and the livery stable facing on the alley between Liberty and

Wood Streets occupied by Joe Melillo. The property occupied as a garage by A. Serville, that occupied by a jewelry store run by A. W. Marg, and the old street car station on Liberty street, were owned by Mrs. Alice Reebel of Edinburg.

Two Churches

The Presbyterian Church at the corner of Second and Wood Street and the Methodist Church located at the corner of third and Wood Street, were destroyed, as was a barn located between the two churches owned by the Struthers Furniture Co. and occupied as a livery stable by J. S. McConnell.

The only buildings in the block left standing were the dwellings of Martin Sheridan in Third Street, which was somewhat isolated from the others and did not take fire, and that of Nick Catone which was saved from fire by the use of dynamite, but was practically ruined by the blast.

C. E. Braatz carried about $5,000 insurance on his property; Nick Catone about $4,000; Dan Steiner about $3,000, and the Struthers Furniture Co., about $2,000. These amounts were estimated.

Giles Gave Alarm

J. E. Giles, a colored man, was awakened by the odor of smoke in his room over the pool room opposite the Harry and Winter Hall building in Liberty Street. He ran to the town building where Marshals Isaac Erskine and W. P. Flickinger were stationed, on the corner of Liberty and Second streets. The officers looked out and saw flames shooting skyward. The alarm was given and the volunteer department turned out.

Chief Frank Westover and his firemen did fine work on turning out promptly, and the mayor of Lowellville, Robert Erskine, joined the fight against the flames which had spread rapidly.

Joseph Melillo's stable was one of the first buildings to ignite. An attempt was made to get into the stable and rescue about 15 horses there, but the rescuers were driven back and the horses perished. Giles' barber shop was next to catch, and from there the flames spread to a restaurant conducted by Mrs. Louis Freeman. Then followed the homes of George Cluse, Frank Barnhardt and Harry Flattery at Liberty and Second Streets.

Braatz and Varley got into Kiefer & Company's saloon before the fire reached there and discovered that cracksmen had evidently been at work. The fire by this time raged fiercely in the saloon. Braatz and Varley were forced to leave. The Serville garage and the jewelry store of A. W. Marg caught and from there the fire swept to the residence of Joe Melillo. This building was dynamited in the hope of checking the conflagration but it was in vain and the Presbyterian church at Wood and Second Streets was soon a mass of flames. It was a total loss before the fire was controlled. The loss totals at least $10,000 with $4,000 insurance. The piano, organ and some other contents of the church were saved.

Steeple Falls on Store

The steeple of this church fell and set fire to the barn of the Struthers Furniture Company. Horses in this building were rescued. East of the building, the M. E. church caught fire. It was impossible to combat the flames with the water available and the dynamite was resorted to again. The ruins after the fall of the building from the blast were consumed by the fire.

This church was built in 1889 and was regarded as a fine edifice. The loss to the congregation is $15,000. The insurance carried was $3,500.

McConnell's bard, big livery, 150 feet long and 75 feet wide, was devoured. It was one of the first buildings to go. Horses and several vehicles were taken out.

Sam DeSalvo's residence and grocery store at Third and Liberty Streets went up in smoke, also the barber shop of Willis Collins and home of John Thorp. Charles E. Braatz owned nearly all these buildings as well as the one occupied by McConnell's livery and Kiefer & Company liquor establishment. He places his loss at $40,000 only partially covered by insurance.

Youngstown Gives Aid

Four companies of apparatus from Youngstown went to Lowellville to help fight the flames and did good work in checking the spread of the conflagration. However, they were terribly handicapped by the lack of water. Great excitement endured while the fire was at its height and streets and yards were filled with household belongings of those fearing the entire village would be destroyed. Street car service was temporarily interrupted. Mike Johns saved his house by valiant efforts. He spread wet blankets on the roof and sparks falling on those blankets quickly died out.

Many Homeless

It was stated that eight families, those of Nick Catone, Herbert Flattery, George Clause, J. Eberhardt, J. Thorp, J. E. Giles, a family named Brown, Willis Collins and Sam DeSalvo, comprising in all about 50 persons, were rendered homeless by the blaze. They all escaped from their residences and buildings consumed by fire with little difficulty, and were cared for at the homes of neighbors. The mother and several children in the Brown family, who resided over Joe Melillo's stable were suffering from the measles.

The fire practically burned itself out. It was pronounced under control about daybreak. However, the ruins still blazed in places at 8 o'clock and a pall of smoke hung over the buildings, which had been lost. All of the structures destroyed were of frame construction.

Historical Footnote: Whatever the cause of the big 1917 fire, it changed the lives of many people. Some after losing everything, like barber Willis Collins, left town and never returned. Others, like Carl Braatz whose loss was estimated at $40,000 in rental property, had no choice but to find a new way to make a living and ended up working long into what should have been an easy retirement. In today's dollars the cost of this fire would have easily exceeded one million dollars.

6 JAIL HOUSE ANTICS

Lowellville's jail or "lock up" provides us with a number of interesting stories about the characters who passed through its doors. The jail was located in the original city hall located on Liberty Street where the current city hall now stands. The former city hall was built in 1871 and torn down in 1934. The original jail had four cells that could hold up to twenty prisoners. It was expanded in 1912 to hold up to forty prisoners in order to meet the demand to hold all the rowdy men who came to Lowellville in search of liquor and other pleasures in the early twentieth century. The village marshal, Tony Fisher, reported that in 1909 there were 1,024 arrests for intoxication and disturbances, and within a few years this number exceeded 1,600 arrests per year.

The jail not only housed prisoners, it also served as hostel of sorts for the tramps who passed through town while riding the rails. Marshal Fisher's 1909 report also showed that 474 tramps found overnight lodging in the village jail that year.

Here is a story about Mayor Porter Watson "kicking butt" …

The Youngstown Vindicator *(Youngstown, OH) published on February 25, 1899:*

MAYOR WATSON, OF LOWELLVILLE, USES HEROIC METHODS AGAINST A HUNGARIAN

A Hungarian with an unpronounceable name, was arrested Monday afternoon for drunkenness, says the **Lowellville Leader**. He was placed in the lock up, and after a few hours of sleep felt himself again. The arresting officer called at the lockup during the afternoon, and the prisoner offered a silver watch as security if permitted to depart. The watch was accepted, turned over to Mayor Watson and the man departed.

Later he called at the post office, and finding the mayor, demanded his watch at once. He was informed that $4.65 was required to redeem the same, that being the amount of the fine and costs. The foreigner became boisterous and abusive but it only took Mayor Watson about two seconds to open the door, and the man wanting the watch, landed on the sidewalk on the point of his honor's shoe. He was taken back to the lockup, then he was released on the following morning.

Historical Footnote: *Porter Watson was not only the mayor at the time of the incident, he was also the postmaster which is why the Hungarian went to the post office to get his watch back. This Porter Watson is the same man who fought John Grist over the "ruin" of his daughter by Grist's son in 1891.*

⌒

Here is a case of mistaken identity and our villagers' desire to be a part of the excitement of an infamous crime, "The Titusville (Pennsylvania) Robbery"… the description of the Lowellville mob in the article that follows is quite colorful! I bet the mistaken robber never came back to Lowellville …

A little background on the Titusville Robbery is necessary so you will understand why folks were so excited about having a suspected robber in their midst. On November 11, 1899 in Titusville, PA three men blew a safe at the Dunkirk, Allegheny Valley and Pittsburgh Railway station and then proceeded to Bertha Bloom's house of ill repute to rob the "inmates" there of their jewelry, money and other valuables. While the robbers were "taking advantage" of the ladies, the Titusville Chief of Police Daniel McGrath and his officer Sheehy were in pursuit. When they arrived at the Bloom house, there was a gun battle and both police officers were shot, McGrath was mortally wounded and died four days later, Sheehy survived. One of the robbers was killed in the shootout (he was never identified), one named Daniel J. Kehoe (alias Frank Major) was captured the same day and eventually hung. The third robber Frank Woodward (alias Frederick Adams) was on the lam and this is whom everyone thought they had in Lowellville. The real Frank Woodward was eventually captured elsewhere and spent time in prison for his part in the crime.

The Youngstown Vindicator *(Youngstown, OH) published on November 21, 1899:*

NOT THE MAN
He Was Locked in a Car and Said to Be a Titusville Desperado
Lowellville Excited and a Mob Gathered, But the Suspect Proved

His Innocence and all is Now Serene

This morning about 7 o'clock Operator Jack McDonough, at the Central police station, was called up by a gentleman in Lowellville who told in an excited voice that they thought they had the Titusville robber who was in the affray that resulted in the death of one of the desperadoes and of Chief of Police McGrath, the tragedy being in the Bloom house, in a sparsely settled portion of town.

The telephone message was to the effect that the supposed robber and murderer was locked in a boxcar and asked to have an officer sent to the Pittsburgh & Western depot here, as it was the intention to run the car into this city and have the authorities here take him out and incarcerate him. The Lowellville party said that the suspect answered the description given of the Titusville man, which the description is as follows:

About 5 feet 8 inches tall; rather heavy set; eyes brown and very small; brown hair, thin on top; brown mustache, curls at the ends; very red cheeks; short nose; even teeth; resembles a German in appearance; wore a red flannel undershirt and blue flannel overshirt; drab socks with white toes and heels; brown slouch hat and brown clothes; blue bow tie with white polka dots; black shoes with heavy broad soles; age, about 35.

A reward of $3,500 has been offered for the capture of the robber, dead or alive.

When the news spread that the desperado was secured in the car, there was great excitement in Lowellville, the populace gathering in short order with guns, pitchforks, fence pickets, pike poles, boat hooks and rolling-pins, making one think of a mob of Frenchmen during the reign of terror. Some of the bolder men in the crowd held a council of war, in which it was decided to make an investigation, which resulted in the decision that suspect was not the wanted man. He showed papers to prove that he was an old soldier and made such a satisfactory showing that he was released.

Lowellville has again settled down to the even tenor of its aristocratic rural monotony.

The Robbers Identified

The name, an excellent photograph and a complete description were obtained at the Erie county (N.Y.) penitentiary today by Crawford county authorities, of the third robber, who is still at large, who participated in the killing of Chief of Police McGrath and the serious wounding of Patrolman Sheehy, of this city, on Saturday morning, November 11.

The fugitive's name is Frank Woodward, alias Frederick Adams. Woodward served three years in the above named institution for taking part in a shooting scrape, being released in September 1896.

Here is another story of mistaken identity in the Lowellville lockup. The suspect in this story was a fugitive named Tom O'Toole. O'Toole was a New Castle man who had murdered his brother-in-law in cold blood in 1905 and was convicted in 1906. Tom appealed the verdict and was incarcerated in the New Castle city jail to wait out a decision on his appeal. Tom being a clever man found a piece of flattened metal and over a period of several weeks began filing away at the bars of his cell each night. After he was able to get from his cell through the cut bars, he found a weak spot in the jail walls and began slowly chiseling out bricks and mortar. He was careful to replace the loosened bricks before returning to his cell in the early morning hours. Tom was able to do this undetected for several weeks. On the morning of August 2, 1906 a county employee noticed loose bricks on the ground near the jailhouse wall, a check of Tom's cell found it still locked but empty. Tom O'Toole was on the loose. Thus in 1907 the hunt for O'Toole was big news.

The New Castle News *(New Castle, PA) published on August 28, 1907:*

LOWELLVILLE OFFICERS THOUGHT THEY HAD THE FUGITIVE, TOM O'TOOLE

Another Tom O'Toole capture scare was sprung late Tuesday afternoon when word reached this city that a prisoner supposed to be O'Toole was behind the bars at Lowellville, O. Detective Mehard and a representative of **The News** immediately went to the Ohio village for the purpose of identifying the prisoner, but to their sorrow, but more to the sorrow of the arresting officers, it was found that the suspect was not the badly wanted fugitive. Yet he was a resident of this city and has been responsible for more excitement early Tuesday morning than the village has witnessed in the past moon, not even excluding the whirl of excitement owing to the street fair which is now holding boards there.

William Green, for that was the name the prisoner gave, stands accused of drunkenness, disorderly conduct and even an attempt to break out of a caboose, which at the best is a poor excuse for a lockup. One, Will Slater, another resident of New Castle, is also in the mix-up and is accused of assisting Green in his attempted escape.

Early Tuesday morning Green was picked up by the Lowellville marshal partially on a charge of suspicion and also because he showed signs of advanced intoxication. It seems that some time before his arrest, Green had stopped a man on the street and because he refused to give him a quarter on demand, had directed a tirade of abuse at him, calling the Lowellvillite anything and everything but a gentleman. This does not go in Ohio, especially when the offender is suspected with being from New Castle, consequently Green bumped into the hard headed dignity of the law and within a short time found himself in vile endurance behind the bars of the lockup. Be it understood that the Lowellville coop is not to be compared with the city prison here. The latter, in comparison, is Sing Sing to the other.

Green's arrest soon became known to another New Castle resident, Will Slater, who was at Lowellville purposely to take in the sights of the street fair. Slater had seen the elephant, had taken a ride on the Ferris wheel and ocean wave and as a finale to his celebration had laid in an oversupply of Lowellville booze. Naturally, when learning of Green's arrest, he interceded on the prisoner's behalf and by a burst of eloquence tried to persuade Mayor Thomas Varley to turn Green loose. But there was no "almost thou persuades me" conviction in Slater's plea, so consequently Mayor Varley turned a deaf ear to his pleadings. But Bill was not content to stop there. He must get Green out.

In explanation it must be stated that the cell in which Green was confined was separated from the mayor's office proper only by a thin partition wall. This fact was known to Green. Slater learned it also. At a time when the mayor's office was deserted, save by himself, Slater by means of an iron poker started to demolish the partition. A hole possibly two inches wide and about two feet long has been made when, he, Mayor Varley put in an appearance. There was a scuffle, lots of confusion and the next scene was portrayed with two New Castle men behind the bars in the place of one. The Good Samaritan act was the undoing of Slater and also wrapped the drag net of the law just a little closer around Green's head. The two Bills were prisoners.

Green appeared very nervous and wanted to get out in the worst kind of a way. This aroused the suspicion of the officers, who thought possibly that his great desire for freedom was prompted by a still greater desire to escape detection on some more serious crime of which he might be guilty and it was here that the O'Toole part of the affair developed.

In general appearance, Green is not altogether unlike O'Toole, although the officers overlooked the fact that O'Toole's hair is light, while that of Green is jet black. This difference, was not noticed until Detective Mehard and a representative of *The News* called the officers' attention to it.

"Well, we've made a mistake," said Mayor Varley, "I see it's not O'Toole but then we are not going to take any chances. It might have been O'Toole and I want to see him captured and would do anything to get him."

The Lowellville officers had taken the right course in the case, as the appearance of Green was such that he might easily be mistaken for the fugitive murderer, barring the difference in the color of hair which would not be noticeable save only to one who was well acquainted with O'Toole.

But even when it was established that the prisoner was not O'Toole, Mayor Varley would not turn him loose, claiming that both Green and Slater had "acted badly", and must suffer. Both men protest innocence of wrong-doing, but admit that in their drunken condition they might have done something that was not in keeping with the "staloots" of Ohio. Which evidently they did.

Mayor Varley accuses Slater of trying to steal a ring which had been taken from a drunk who has been arrested. Slater was in the Mayor's office when the prisoner was brought in and while he was being searched. The ring was laid on the table and while the drunk was being put in a cell Mayor Varley claims that Slater "mouthed" the ring and attempted to escape. Slater denies this.

Green did not know that he was suspected of being O'Toole and to a representative of *The News* jokingly suggested that he tell Mayor Varley that he (Green) was in reality the genuine O'Toole.

"Make them believe they have something big," said Green, "they've treated me mean and I want to get even with them. These Lowellville cops are bad ones. Why one of them reached through the bars while I was asleep and punched me in the face, but I'll get even for that."

As the suspected O'Toole, Green was viewed by scores of excited Lowellville residents, who flocked about the cell just to get a glimpse of the prisoner.

The real Tom O'Toole is still at liberty. Green threatens a damage suit against the borough.

Historical Footnote: In another interesting twist to this story, as late as 1911 a man who had been hit by a train in Lowellville was said to have told a nurse as he was dying that his name was Tom O'Toole. The story caused the public to once again wonder whether Tom O'Toole, the fugitive, had been found. Some wanted to exhume the body but in the end the train accident victim was left to rest in his grave in potter's field at Youngstown's Oak Hill cemetery and the truth about what happened to Tom was never uncovered. Some believed he went to Ireland or traveled as far south as the Panama Canal, but two things are certain, he got away with murder and for one day in 1907 he caused a bit of excitement for the village of Lowellville when he wasn't even there.

Here is a humorous story about one of the village's jailbreaks. This incident forced the village to seriously consider improving the jail to keep inmates in.

The Vindicator *(Youngstown, OH) published on August 14, 1911:*

JAIL DELIVERY
Eight Prisoners Get Out of the Joke Jail at Lowellville
Minor Offenders Were Recaptured Without Much Difficulty - May Mean Better Prison

A daring jail delivery occurred at Lowellville Sunday morning about three o'clock, when eight prisoners broke out of the village lockup. Freedom did not prove any temptation to one of the men, Charles Pender, arrested on a minor charge. When he gained the outside of the old bastille he sat down on a box and commenced to whittle a stick. He was at this occupation when Night Officers Tony Fisher and Jack Crissinger returned in to report after making their rounds.

The two officers, after hearing Pender's story, gave an alarm. Nearly all of the fugitives held on charges of drunkenness were re-captured. William Miller, charged with breaking into a tool house of the Pennsylvania company, and Albert Pender, charged with the theft of a dozen razors, and both liable to workhouse sentences, made good their escape and no trace of them was found. The prisoners re-captured stated that Miller had engineered the jail delivery. He secured an old pocket knife and using the blades as a screwdriver, detached the lock on the front door, and the rest was easy. Pender and Miller made off together after bidding their comrades farewell. The latter is reported to have been amused at the easy manner in which he turned the trick that set the whole bunch at liberty.

Pennsylvania company detectives have all been notified and will keep a sharp lookout for Miller, who is considered a man with a bad record.

Mayor Erskine believes now that means will be taken by the village authorities to make the lockup more secure.

When Lawrence County, Pennsylvania and nearby Struthers, Ohio went dry, the impact on Lowellville was quite notable as reported in the article below ...

The Beaver Falls Tribune *(Beaver Falls, PA) published on August 20, 1912:*

NEW LOCKUP IS BUILT FOR DRUNKS FROM NEW CASTLE

Unable to properly take care of the large number of New Castle men who come here on Saturday nights and indulge so freely that their arrests follow, the village of Lowellville has found it necessary to enlarge its lockup.

The prison, which can now accommodate only twenty persons, will be made large enough to take care of twice that many. Three new cells are being put in and they will be completed by next week.

With the addition of more prison space, the unheard practice of first fining and then discharging drunk men to be arrested the same night again will be abolished, it is thought. In order to make room for the numberless men that are arrested, some nights it is necessary for the burgess of the town to be on the job all the time and fine drunks and "shove them back" into the street while they are still in a sad state of intoxication.

Lowellville, until New Castle went saloonless, was one of the most quiet little towns in eastern Ohio or western Pennsylvania. But after the judge of Lawrence county decreed that the saloons must go, conditions here changed and today Lowellville is one of the rowdiest towns in the state. In the downtown section there are saloons on every corner, the streets are filled with drunken men and the lockup is usually filled also.

Not all of the men who go to make this condition of affairs so repulsive to the good citizens of Lowellville, come from New Castle, but a majority do. Passenger business on the Mahoning Valley lines between New Castle and Lowellville has doubled since the saloons went out of business in the Pennsylvania city, so it can be seen that New Castle money is most exclusively being used to enrich the saloonkeepers of Lowellville and give the town a reputation that will stick to it forever.

Before New Castle went dry, two policemen composed the local force, one in the daytime and the other at night. Now there are three in the daytime with the same number at night, with the entire force working Saturday nights, when the rush is great.

The strong arm of the law endeavors to make the town as orderly as possible, but with a thousand drinking men spending their two weeks' pay, this is no easy task.

Any Saturday night finds the lockup filled up at 10 o'clock. Then the burgess is forced to empty it to make room for some more. He holds Saturday night police court and the prisoners reeling drunkenly before the bar of justice, are found guilty.

"One dollar and costs, $4.85 in all," the burgess drones monotonously, and the money is paid.

The air ranks heavy with the smell of vile whiskey and the curses of the drunks, intermingled with the voice of the burgess, makes the scene most unusual.

Minus the money that they are forced to pay to obtain their freedom, the men stagger back into the saloons and often they are arrested again the very same night.

Those who have no money to pay are forced to work on the streets. The village has white uniforms which the prisoners are forced to wear. Guards watch them as they labor on the highways here.

Between 1905 and 1916, Antonio Rossilano better known as Tony "Italian Bearcat" Ross was a famous prizefighter from New Castle, PA. During his career he fought 75 bouts and had a knock out percentage of 27%. Tony was born around 1885 in Italy and died on August 31, 1941. In 1912 he ended up before Lowellville Mayor Roller for fighting in one of our local saloons. As a result of this altercation and the resulting injuries he received in Lowellville, one of Tony's bouts, scheduled the following month in Cleveland, Ohio, against Jack (Twin) Sullivan had to be called off.

The New Castle News *(New Castle, PA) published on January 19, 1912:*

TONY WAS FINED $40 AND COSTS
Given Financial Hook to Jaw by Lowellville Mayor

Tony Ross, the heavyweight prize fighter from New Castle and a friend by the name of Carrigan, came to Lowellville Wednesday for a sleigh ride. They were accompanied by their wives. It is alleged that Ross accused Cluse, proprietor of the Tip Top Cafe, with insulting Mrs. Ross. The charge was resented and a fight ensued. The police were called. Ross was told to keep quiet and replied he was able to defend and back up any statement he had made. The police decided to arrest Ross, who showed fight. The officers used their maces and Ross suffered several cuts on the head. He and his friends were taken to the police station on a disturbance charge. A doctor was called to attend the wounds on the pug's head. The women members of the Ross party were provided lodging for the night. Thursday afternoon Ross and Carrigan were arraigned before Mayor Roller. Ross was fined $40 and costs and Carrigan $75 and costs, as the evidence showed Carrigan was more to blame for the trouble than Tony. The accused men paid their fines and left Lowellville for New Castle.

Historical Footnote: The newspaper account states that the proprietor of the Tip Top Café was a man named Cluse, his full name was George L. Cluse. Cluse, in 1917, was a bar tender for The John Keifer Company, which was destroyed in the 1917 fire that also destroyed Cluse's home. In the early 1920s Cluse gave up tending bar and became a Lowellville Patrolman. He died on December 11, 1929.

7 THIEVERY

Many of us who grew up in Lowellville remember when it was not unusual to leave our doors unlocked at night ... that Lowellville is not the one you will read about in these stories.

Prior to a bank being established in Lowellville in 1905, many businesses kept cash and other valuables in on premise safes. As a result there were a number of safe cracking incidents.

Money was not always the prize in the burglaries, sometimes it was booze, olive oil, cheese or livestock such as chickens or horses.

Here is a story where only a portion of the stolen "goods" were recovered, but it was evident where the rest of the goods went, even though the thieves did their best to get rid of the evidence!

The Cleveland Leader *(Cleveland, Ohio) published on November 22, 1882:*

Patrick Gauley, Dolmar Gallagher, and Samuel McCluskey were lodged in jail today charged with burglarizing the saloon of J. J. Williamson, Lowellville, this county, at an early hour yesterday morning. When arrested they were drunk from the effects of the stolen liquor they had imbibed. Gauley was at one time a resident of this city, the other prisoners being strangers. Upon being searched at the jail, some of the stolen property was found in their possession.

Here is a story about biting the hand that robs you...

The Plain Dealer *(Cleveland, OH) published on March 25, 1885:*

IDENTIFYING HIS ASSAILANTS

J. H. Brannon, the A & P station agent at Lowellville who was assaulted and robbed by two highwaymen one night last week, was in the city yesterday afternoon. He went to the county jail and had a look at Bobby Gay, who was arrested early Saturday morning on the suspicion of being one of Brannon's assailants, but failed to identify him. He says that one of the tramps, who is an evil-looking fellow, is about the build of one of the men who assaulted him, but that the resemblance practically ends there. He sank his teeth onto the hand of one of his assailants. The tramp has a fresh wound on one of his hands which he says he received a few days ago by a fall. Brannon says one of his assailants threatened to cut his throat with a razor because he had bitten him.

*Historical Footnote: Even though Brannon could not positively identify Bobby Gay as his assailant, Gay eventually pleaded guilty to the assault. In a subsequent newspaper article in **The Plain Dealer**, it was reported, "James Lalley and Robert Gay, who pleaded guilty to knocking Station Agent Brannon of Lowellville down with a coupling pin and robbing him, were each sentenced to eight years' imprisonment... there were some affecting scenes in court. Lalley broke down and cried like a child."*

Everyone has heard of horse thieves ... here is a story of a horse thief who also had a fondness for stealing chickens too. The John Igo in this story was the son of John Igo, who you read about earlier -- the elder Igo being the man who was shot by his grandson for abusing Mrs. Igo.

The Youngstown Vindicator *(Youngstown, OH) published on October 9, 1902:*

BAD RECORD
Of the Chicken Thief Known to Police - Right Name is John Igo Has Been Wanted for a Year for Horse Stealing and Will Be Indicted on That Charge

Chief McDowell, when he interviewed "Fred Baker", the alleged chicken thief, in the lock-up Thursday morning, discovered that Officers Kane and Hartenstein had arrested John Igo of Lowellville, wanted since the 19th of October 1901, for horse stealing.

The warrant for Igo, arrested on the horse stealing charge was sworn out by William Seidner. Igo took Seidner's horse and buggy from the rear of McKelvey's store on the date in question and drove the horse to Warren. In Warren he sold the buggy to a hotel proprietor for $5 and was about to dispose of the horse when he learned that the police were after him. He then vamoosed and left the horse in a livery barn at Warren, where it was recovered, together with the buggy, by the owner.

Igo who gave the name of Fred Baker this morning, told the chief that the chickens he was selling at such reduced figures, belonged to his mother, and that he was told to dispose of them for her. He said that he had been drinking and for that reason was late in getting into town, and drink may have been responsible also for the ridiculous price he was asking for the poultry. He said that the chickens he had sold a few days ago were the property of his sister. He declared positively that he was telling the truth about the chickens, but the chief knows that the story is false. However, the chicken stealing is the least crime for which Igo will have to answer, as a grand jury will be given the facts in the horse stealing case today, and a true bill will likely be returned, for Igo, who this morning admitted that he had stolen the buggy and that he had simply received $5 for the same.

Igo is a tall man and is well known to this department. He was known to be in the vicinity of Lowellville, but for some time after he had been located after the horse stealing episode, he was ill at the home of a relative in Pennsylvania, just across the state line, and no effort was made to get him back at that time, for it was believed that he would be in Lowellville as soon as he recovered.

The crate of chickens which Igo had with him this morning was sent to the police station by the police officer who made the arrest, and the fowls are at the patrol barn. The chief hopes to learn from whom the chickens were taken when the facts of the arrest reach the farmers in the vicinity of Lowellville.

The clever work of Kane and Hartenstein is in line with their past records in this respect, and is very pleasing to the department as well as Chief McDowell.

Historical Footnote: *John E. Igo was born in September 1875. Baker, the alias he used, was his mother's maiden name. Apparently John was a career thief, at the time when he was trying to pass himself off as Fred Baker, he was on the lam from New Castle, PA. While in jail there, he had escaped and financed his freedom by stealing a sack of flour!*

The Indiana Democrat *(Indiana, PA) published May 21, 1902:*

John Igo, a Lowellville man who was serving a 60 day sentence in jail at New Castle escaped from that institution, stole flour from a wholesale grocery establishment, which he then sold to secure money to leave the city and has disappeared.

William Smith was a new merchant in town when his business was robbed …

The Youngstown Vindicator *(Youngstown, OH) published on November 22, 1907:*

BOLD ROBBERY AT LOWELLVILLE
Thieves Enter the Store of William Smith Thursday Night and Make Off With Goods Valued at $800
Took Gent's Furnishing Goods Enough to Half Fill a Moving Van – No Clue Yet Discovered

The authorities are now hard at work on the boldest and most baffling burglary in the history of Lowellville with little or no possibility of a chance of apprehending the men who late Thursday night entered the store of William Smith in the Erskine block and made off with goods valued from $700 to $800.

Entrance to the building was gained by prying open a window in the back of the store. Once inside, the men, at least two in number and possibly three, forced open the door to make it easier to get away with their plunder. They took enough gents' furnishing goods to fill half a van, and it is believed by the authorities that a wagon was used to take the stolen goods away.

Mr. Smith discovered the burglary when he came down Friday morning to unlock his store. He took a hasty inventory, and said later that his loss would probably exceed $700. There is nothing about the place that will enable the authorities to apprehend the burglars. Constable George Rastus, Marshal William Baker and Mayor Varley are all working to solve the robbery. They have telephoned to nearby towns and cities, but at noon today had not received any word regarding the whereabouts of the burglars.

Historical Footnote: *William Smith had a terrible run of misfortune that* *culminated with this robbery. A year earlier he had moved his family and his business from New Castle, PA to Lowellville thinking that a new location and a new start would improve his family's luck. While in New Castle he lost a daughter when she died from burns, another daughter, Dorothy, fell down a flight of steps and suffered a traumatic brain injury and was said to be demented and his New Castle hardware store burned to the ground. However, tragedy followed Smith across the state line when his 18 year old daughter, Lilly, drowned in the Mahoning River on the night of the Mt. Carmel Festival's fireworks in July 1907.*

Smith's store was located at 224 Water Street and he remained in business for two decades. In 1927, he sold the store to his son-in-law, Sam Simon. Sam and his wife, Tillie Smith Simon, operated "Sam Simon's" in that location until their retirement in 1972.

One of the Mahoning Limestone Company's operations was located at one time just outside of the village limits on East Wood Street near the Ohio-Pennsylvania state line. Eventually the operation was abandoned on the property and the land and buildings located on it were rented out. In 1931, my grandparents, Antonio and Giovanna Torella purchased the land, house and barn for $1,800 from the Mahoning Limestone Company and today it is still in our family.

In 2012 we had soil testing done for a new septic system and were told by the tester that he believed that there has been some sort of limestone processing done on the property at least a 100 years ago and this was without him knowing about the property's history. After reading the article below, I am wondering if the watchman's shanty eventually became the home that I grew up in. While doing remodeling in the 1970s we discovered log walls in the original section of the house and an old yard stick bearing the name The Mahoning Limestone Company.

The New Castle News *(New Castle, PA) published on December 16, 1908:*

TRAMPS THROW OUT WATCHMAN

Two negro tramps Monday night took possession of the watchman's shanty at the crusher of the Mahoning Limestone Co. near Lowellville, where Robert Osborne was in charge. The two men ate Mr. Osborne's lunch, took all of his tobacco and a gold ring from him, after throwing him out of the place; made themselves comfortable and went to sleep.

Here is story about a number of home robberies and attempted robberies. Two of the family names will be familiar as I had earlier shared a story about a young Thomas Driscoll who was accused of assaulting Cora Della Rentz back in 1895. Well, eighteen years later, the Driscoll and Rentz families made the news again. Both of their homes were targeted among others in the village. Thomas Driscoll, was now a village police officer living in the village near the Rentz family. It's hard to keep one's enemies far away in a small village like Lowellville.

The Youngstown Vindicator *(Youngstown, OH) published on July 12, 1913:*

LOWELLVILLE

Burglars gained entrance to several homes here Thursday evening, among them being the home of Fred Lantz of East Wood Street, which was entered sometime after midnight and robbed of a number of valuable pieces of jewelry, a gold watch and necklace belonging to Miss Bertha Lantz; also a small sum of money belonging to the Presbyterian church, that Miss Lantz had in her keeping. Miss Lantz was asleep in the room with the lights burning and was never awakened by the robbers. They gained entrance through a window and left by the front door leaving the door wide open. They also visited the home of Night Policeman Thomas Driscoll, but nothing was taken, they having overlooked a box containing jewelry and valuable papers. They tried to gain entrance to the homes of Henry Rentz and Mr. Phillips of East Wood Street but were frightened away. It is thought that perhaps the robbers might been the three colored men who attacked Peter Hill, an employee of Edward Scanlon early Thursday evening while he was going from town to the tents in West Wood Street. His cries for help brought fellow workmen to his assistance, but not however, before he was badly beaten.

This next story has me wondering if at least one of the burglars was Italian considering their choice of goods to steal ... a 1/2 dozen bottles of olive oil and some cheese were gathered in a basket but which were ultimately left behind.

The Youngstown Vindicator *(Youngstown, OH) published on November 27, 1915:*

VILLAGE STORE BURGLARIZED
Goods Valued at Several Hundred Dollars Taken in Lowellville

Goods estimated at $200 in value were stolen from the grocery and hardware store of Andrew Kroeck on Water Street in Lowellville some time Friday night. Two fine repeating shotguns, one single-barreled shotgun, one automobile lap robe, six horse blankets and six or eight razors were the articles taken.

A basket, which was in the store, was filled with groceries by the thieves but was not taken. Police officers of Lowellville believe that the intruders either became frightened and left the groceries or that they did not want to carry them. In the basket were a half dozen bottles of olive oil, several pounds of cheese and some canned goods.

Entrance was gained by smashing the glass in one of the side panels of the front window, near the front door. Absolutely no tracks could be found within the store or outside. Two night policemen were on duty but they saw no prowlers or suspicious looking characters. It is the belief of the officers that the work was done by professionals, as apparently great care was taken to effect an entrance to the store when the officers were in other parts of town. It is also believed that the robbery was committed in a very short space of time.

The store building is owned by Mr. Kroeck. The Lowellville opera house occupies one section of the building. The structure is located in the main business section of Lowellville.

Historical Footnote: This was Andrew Kroeck's first store in Lowellville. He had purchased a hardware business from Frank Leish in 1906 in the village opera house. The "Opera House" was a large three story building with the Kroeck hardware store on the first floor, storage on the second floor and space for entertainment and lodge meetings on the third floor. In 1919 Andrew built a new building located at 219 E. Wood Street and in 1920 sold out his hardware business. At the Wood Street building he went into the automobile business and sold Ford Model Ts. Eventually his son, Arthur Kroeck took over his business and operated a gas station and hardware store at the location until his retirement in 1976. Arthur sold his business to Robert Giovanni Sr. who operated it until it was destroyed by fire in the early 1990s.

Below are a series of three articles that describe a Wild West type robbery and shoot out that occurred near Lowellville which resulted in the deaths of several men. Stories of the shooting made headlines across the nation …

The Youngstown Vindicator *(Youngstown, Ohio) published on November 16, 1917:*

LOWELLVILLE

George James of this place was in the automobile held up by bandits on the Edinburg hill Thursday afternoon when Bert Farrell, former Lowellville man, was shot three times and the other man in the seat with him was killed instantly by a shot in the head and the holdups got away with the Johnston quarry payroll amounting to thousands of dollars. Later one of the holdup men was found dead about a half mile away from where the robbery was committed.

A subsequent article from **The Youngstown Vindicator** *(Youngstown, OH) published on November 16, 1917:*

ONE BANDIT IS KILLED, SECOND CAUGHT IN TREE
Holdup Near Hillsville Staged in True Wild West Fashion
Robbers Slay Young Italian in Pay Car
Men with Payroll for Johnston Quarry Battle Bravely – Part of Stolen $17,000 Recovered – Two Robbers Escape

As a result of the daring holdup Thursday afternoon of the paymaster and superintendent of the Johnston Limestone quarries at Hillsville, two men are dead, one bandit, while two others are at the Shenango Valley hospital in New Castle, one a bandit, both seriously wounded. The news of the holdup was contained in the **Vindicator** Thursday afternoon.

The dead are Tony Sacco, a young man of Hillsville, who was the occupant of the automobile containing the money, and a bandit believed to be Mike Garlich.

There is supposition that Garlich may have been shot down by his companions in a quarrel over the division of the loot.

The injured at the hospital are A. D. Farrell, superintendent at the quarries, and Moyek Zorko, giving his residence as Lowellville, O. He was chased by the posse summoned by George James, who, escaping from the bandits ran to Hillsville for assistance. Zorko was found hiding in a tall tree, and was shot before he had time to draw his gun.

Too Weak To Talk

At New Castle Friday, it is stated that Farrell was too weak to talk about the holdup. Zorko, who is not fatally injured, positively refuses to say anything about the robbery.

It is also stated that $9,700 of the $17,000 stolen has been recovered. Two of the bandits who made good their escape from the posse are still being hunted. They have the balance of the money. The Lawrence county authorities expect to get such information from Zorko today that will enable them to locate the other two bandits. At Lowellville where Zorko says he resided, the police do not know anything about him. The Lowellville officers stated today that from what they can learn, Zorko, is an Austrian.

The holdup was cleverly planned and carried out in true Western style. George James and A. D. Farrell, officials of the Johnston Limestone quarries, journeyed as usual on paydays to New Castle to get the money for the large payroll. The trip was made in an automobile and both men were armed with revolvers.

Returning early in the afternoon, the trip to Edinburg was made without an incident of any kind. On leaving Edinburg and crossing to the south side of the river, the officials picked up Tony Sacco, one of the Italian employees at the quarries, aged about 20 years. He was walking towards Hillsville.

As the automobile party left the roadway that runs parallel with the Pennsylvania tracks and commenced to ascend the long incline at Hillsville, four men sprung out of the woods and pointing guns at Farrell and his companions, demanded surrender. Farrell answered with a volley of shots, and a regular battle followed.

When Farrell had been shot down and Tony Sacco killed, James still unharmed made off to Hillsville for help. Returning with a posse, Matt Garlic's body was found 300 feet from the where the holdup occurred.

On the person of the dead bandit $4,000 was found. The posse then chased and ran down Zorko, who was captured at the top of a tree, which he had climbed. On his person was found $5,700. Several hundred men had joined in the search when Zorko was caught. He was shot down before he had a chance to draw his gun.

After Matt Garlic known in East Youngstown as Mike Garlich, was shot and killed, a pay check of the Youngstown Sheet and Tube Co. was found on his person. W. J. Edwards, special police officer in Hillsville, on securing this information took the man's pay check number and hastened to East

Youngstown. At the mill the officer learned the man occupied rooms over Goddard's saloon.

Search Bandit's Room

With Patrolman Putka, of the East Youngstown force, Edwards went to Garlich's room. Here he found a valise belonging to the dead bandit, which contained a box of cartridges of the caliber fitting the automatic revolver found with the body at Hillsville. Also a photograph of the deceased, which Edwards took back to Hillsville with him.

An attempt will be made to discover if Garlich had a criminal record and if so, the identity of his two companions who escaped may be discovered. This will be necessary if Zorko, the Lowellville bandit at the Shenango Valley hospital at New Castle, maintains his silence regarding the details of the holdup.

Two From Detroit

Marshall James Murray of East Youngstown who has investigated the case from this end, says that some time ago Mike Garlich, giving his former residence as New York and Mike Kovak and Boza Draskovich, the latter two of Detroit, took up their residence at Stop 11 ½. The men acted suspiciously and attracted the attention of the East Youngstown police. The men did not mix with other countrymen, and spent most of their time in and around Struthers.

Plan the Holdup

It is the opinion of the police that the three men took up with Moyek Zorko of Lowellville. Then the four planned the holdup. Zorko is now at the Shenango Valley hospital under guard, Mike Garlich is dead, and Mike Kovak and Boza Draskovich are at large with a large posse from Hillsville scouring the adjacent country for them.

The two men at large are each about 21 years of age. They have several thousand dollars with them secured from the holdup. Police officers from all of the surrounding towns have been alerted and it is the belief of the company and county officials that they will be eventually captured. An effort to secure the whereabouts of the two men who are away, and their rooms are being carefully searched. All of Thursday night, the East Youngstown police watched the house where the trio of bandits had lived but the fugitive outlaws failed to show up.

Here is the third article in the series where the police believed that they had caught one of the bandits that was on the loose...

The Youngstown Vindicator *(Youngstown, OH) published 19, 1917:*

DESIRE TO SEE DEAD PAL PROVES UNDOING OF KOVAK
Trailed From Morgue and Landed in County Jail Here – Buried Money Under Slaughterhouse – Refuses to Talk – Pinkerton Makes Catch

With the capture Saturday evening at 7:30 o'clock in East Youngstown of Paul Kovak, only two of the bandits who held up A. D. Farrell and George James, superintendent and paymaster of the Johnston Limestone quarries at Hillsville, Thursday, are now at large. With the finding of $600 of the missing money under the floors at an old slaughterhouse, 500 yards from the scene of the holdup, $14,000 of the $17,000 has been recovered.

Saturday Kovak showed up in New Castle visiting the morgue where Michael Garlich's remains were and asked to see the body. Identifying the body as that of his former pal, Kovak journeyed to the Shenango Valley hospital and asked to see Moyek Zorko, a patient there under heavy guard and suspected of being an accomplice in the holdup.

Zorko greeted Kovak with an oath. He charged his pal of Thursday afternoon with being disloyal and bungling up on the job. The New Castle police were not notified, so Kovak, becoming bolder went back to his boarding house on Stop 11 ½ East Youngstown. J. J. O'Toole, a Pinkerton detective from the Pittsburgh office, detailed to run down the escaped bandits, upon learning of Kovak's movements followed him to East Youngstown, where with Sergeant John Putko of the village police force, he arrested the alleged bandit as he sat in front of a stove at Welsh's boarding house over George Goddard's saloon.

Kovak was taken by the two officers to the East Youngstown lockup where he was searched, $43 being found on his person. He positively refused to talk about the holdup, being very reticent and surly. Detective O'Toole with Sergeant Putko accompanied Kovak to the county jail here where the prisoner is lodged. The Pinkerton representative states that in his opinion Kovak got "cold feet" and feeling remorseful at the death of his pal, Mike Garlich, became desperate and did not fear capture.

Were in California

The officers through the Pinkerton agency have learned that Paul Kovak and Michael Garlich sojourned for three or four years in California. Then they came east together. Kovak at one time was employed at the Johnston Limestone quarries.

Detective O'Toole says that Mike Garlich was shot and killed by one of his pals. The four bandits were in wait along the Hillsville road fully an hour before A. D. Farrell and George James came along. J. S. Weaver, representative for R. G. Dunn in Youngstown came along the lonesome roadway 15 minutes ahead of the paymaster and his party. The bandits stopped his automobile and searched it, supposing he was a representative of the Johnston Limestone Co. He was permitted to go on unharmed.

Mike Garlich who had mounted the running board of the automobile received a bullet in the leg that severed an artery. Undaunted Garlich grabbed up two shoe boxes containing the $9,000 from the car and ran towards the old slaughterhouse. His pals took the other boxes. The bandits had planned to pair up, two men to travel in a different direction. Garlich, bleeding from a severed artery, fell in a clump of bushes. He died there. Zorko who was to go with him, missing his companion, climbed up a tree in an attempt to locate him. It was here the posse found him.

When Zorko refused to descend, two shots were fired by members of the posse over his head. Then he was given a bullet that pierced his shoulder. His left arm has been amputated by surgeons at the Shenango Valley hospital.

Detective O'Toole believes that the four bandits are amateurs at the holdup game. He says, however, that Paul Kovak and Mike Garlich may have been in other scrapes in the West. Boza Draskovich and Gravil Korzal, the bandits now at large, will be captured, believes Detective O'Toole, who went back to New Castle Saturday night.

Historical Footnote: It didn't take long for detectives to realize that Kovak was not one of the bandits and that he was merely visiting his friend. Months went by and the two escaped bandits had still not been caught. Meanwhile, former Lowellville resident, Moyek Zorko, stood trial for the murder of Antonio "Tony" Sacco. His trial lasted three days and after three hours of deliberation, he was found guilty of first degree murder on Christmas eve 1917. With a murder conviction, he faced the death penalty and he immediately appealed his conviction with the defense that he was unarmed during the robbery. He remained in the county jail while his request for a new trial was pending.

Based on tips from the Austrian immigrant community a break in the case finally came for the Lawrence County police. Two of the suspects, they were told, were working under assumed names near Pottsville, Pennsylvania. Immediately Lawrence County sent four officers to round up the suspects. The first suspect was Gravil Korzal who was found at his workplace, a Pennsylvanian coal mine in Tuscaroa, shoveling coal and using the name John Sellers. Sixty miles away at virtually the same time, half of the Lawrence County officer contingent went after a farm laborer using the name of George Millish but who was really Boza Draskovich. Draskovich was found at a farm hitching up a team of horses and was easily apprehended. Both men told their captors that they were tired of being on the run and immediately confessed to taking part in the holdup. By the time they were caught, neither of the two men had any of the $4,100 in payroll money still missing. Both were brought to Lawrence County. Their co-conspirator, Zorko, who had been steadfast in his silence and lack of cooperation, was worn down from his incarceration, perhaps it was added of trauma of losing an arm and suffering from tuberculosis, that allowed him to readily identify the two men. The case against the men seemed to be pretty strong with their confessions and identification by both Zorko and Bert Farrell, the other shooting victim. It was expected that Lawrence County would have two more death penalty cases.

Korzal admitted to firing two shots but claimed that it was the other bandit, found dead at the scene, Garlich who did most of the shooting. Draskovich would not admit to doing any shooting but only that he was there that day on the hill and took the money. Both men stated that Garlich accidentally shot himself while jumping over a fence.

The men told of how they split up the $2,600 that they had absconded with and used the money to travel to Warren, Cleveland, Detroit and then finally returning to Pennsylvania where they went their separate ways. After seven months on the lam—neither man's life in America was any better than it was before the holdup. Ironically, Korzal lost the last of his holdup money - $900 - to an unsavory character who beat him and stole the money. After accounting for their share, $1,500 from the original $17,000 still remained missing and was never accounted for.

Korzal was the first of the pair to go on trial and in July 1918, he was found guilty of manslaughter. The judge was not pleased with the jury's decision as he believed the evidence pointed to first degree murder as the county had already successfully secured a murder conviction for Zorko for the same incident. However, he stated that he "would endeavor to do his duty" and he sentenced Korzal based on the lesser charge. Korzal escaped the death penalty and was sentenced to at least 23 years but no more than 29 years in the Western Penitentiary. In September 1918, Draskovitch went on trial charged with first degree murder. Amazingly his jury found him guilty of the murder charge and the judge ordered him to be sentenced to death. On March 1, 1920 Draskovitch was electrocuted at the Rockview Penitentiary in Centre County, PA and was buried there. Less than a month later, Moyek Zorko succumbed to tuberculosis on

March 29, 1920 at the Lawrence County jail still awaiting his request for a new trial to save himself from the electric chair. In the end five lives were ruined and the American dream for four young Austrian immigrants turned into a nightmare by their own folly. The death of Tony Sacco, the innocent young man, who just wanted a ride to work, was particularly pitiful.

A story of an unwanted house call from a plumber ...

The Plain Dealer *(Cleveland, OH) published on April 10, 1919:*

ALLEGED INTRUDER SHOT
Entered Lowellville Home by Breaking Window, Woman Says

Alleged to have entered the home of Barney Maloney at Lowellville today, a man giving the name of John Graham was shot and wounded in the legs by Frank Curry, brother-in-law of Mr. Maloney, who resides in an adjoining house, authorities say. The man was brought to Youngstown hospital by the Lowellville police, who are investigating the case, in his pocket was a plumber's card which had been issued at Akron.

Mrs. Maloney and a child, who were alone in the house heard the intruder attempt to enter a rear door. Failing in this, he went to the front of the house and broke a pane of glass in the door, after which he entered the house, removed his coat and started to wash himself. Screams of the woman attracted Curry.

Historical Footnote: Mrs. Maloney was the former Dorothy "Dot" Mortimer and the child with her during the incident was her young son, 3 ½ year old Eugene. The incident occurred at their home on Jackson Street. There was an error in the original article, it listed Frank as the son-in-law of Barney and Dot Maloney. Frank was married to Dot's sister, Maye.

8 DISREPUTABLE HOUSES

Lowellville had its fair share of "disreputable" houses and the ladies who worked in these houses were politely referred to in the newspapers of the time as "inmates". Here are a few articles about these "disorderly houses", their customers and inmates.

In 1902 there was a crackdown on Lowellville's "disorderly" houses ...

The New Castle News *(New Castle, PA) published on September 24, 1902:*

ARE RAIDING VICE IN LOWELLVILLE

There is disposition evidenced by the residents of some of the village officials at Lowellville to rid the town of disorderly houses, says the **Youngstown Vindicator** of Thursday. Mayor T. J. Whitmer of Lowellville had two of the proprietresses of the alleged places before him yesterday and arraigned them on charges which were sworn to by a number of residents.

Both of the women pleaded not guilty. The mayor bound them over to court and they, being unable to furnish bail and having no person to befriend them, were placed in the county jail.

One of the Italian houses that has been the scene of many disgraceful affairs was abated last week because of a quarrel between the proprietress and the inmate who eloped with a Sharon man and against whom the proprietress brought an action for grand larceny, charging the eloping couple with the theft of $103.50. It is stated that all of these places were rendezvous for the low characters of the community.

Here's an article that scolds the same mayor from the article above for attempting to protect the identities of some young men who came from the "fine" families of Lowellville who had earlier caused a scene at a house of "ill fame".

The Youngstown Vindicator *(Youngstown, OH) published on June 10, 1904:*

HIS HONOR
Mayor Whitmer, of Lowellville, in Role of Press Censor
Afraid of Aristocrats

Withholds Names of Men Arrested for Rioting – What if They Were Poor Devils

"It wouldn't do to print their names, anyway" was the remark of Mayor Thomas Whitmer of Lowellville as he concluded a long search this morning through his desk seeking, or pretending to seek an affidavit which has been filed by Mamie Morris charging six young men of that borough with disorderly conduct. "They belong to the very best families in the town and – well, it would cause an awful fuss to print their names. They might come out at the hearing Wednesday morning, but they will probably settle the case before they permit it to go to trial if they know there is any likelihood of newspaper notoriety."

The mayor was speaking of a case that has attracted a great deal of attention. It was to have been heard this morning, but because there was a funeral in town that demanded the attention of several of the people necessary to the trial, and because of other reasons, the case was continued by consent of all parties.

The charge of disorderly conduct was filed by Mamie Morris, alleged to be the proprietress of Lowellville's only house of ill fame. The six young men who she names, were in her place on Friday evening, June 3, it is alleged in the missing affidavit, and there raised a rough house. The "riot" as it is termed by Attorney John Roller, who represents the complainant, Miss Morris, attracted so much attention that on the following Sunday evening, the house was pulled. Marshal Baker got several visitors, the proprietress, and one girl. Morris was fined $10 and costs, the girl $5 and costs, and each of the visitors $1 and costs.

None of these visitors were the scions of the families of the elite who had participated in the "riot" on the evening of June 3. Miss Morris was sore on the pull and everybody connected with it, and declared her belief that the young men, who had put the house to the bad previously, were responsible for the pull. She thereupon swore out an information charging them with the disorder.

It is this hearing that is booked for Wednesday morning because of the continuance from this morning.

Another "disorderly house" story ... sensational disclosures were promised, but unfortunately for us none could be found in the newspapers published after this initial report ...

The New Castle News *(New Castle, PA) published on May 22, 1915:*

WILL AIR CHARGES AGAINST OFFICERS

Joe Sparigo was fined $150 and costs and Lillian Carter $50 and costs Friday afternoon by Mayor Erskine. Sparigo was charged with running a disorderly house and the Carter woman being an inmate.

Lillian Carter says the raid made on Sparigo's house was the result of a political frame-up and charges made by Marshal Tony Fisher against officers Roy Niggel and Mont Boyle, it is said, will be presented to A. M. Henderson, prosecuting attorney, Saturday morning. It is said some sensational disclosures will be made.

In this incident there were three people arrested in the house - two ladies and one man ... and the only two who received sentences and ended up with a record and named in the newspaper were the "ladies" ... without knowing all the details, however, it does seem a little unfair to me ...

The Youngstown Vindicator *(Youngstown, OH) published on March 30, 1916:*

WOMAN IS GIVEN A SEVERE FINE
Mrs. Mary Ryan, of Lowellville, committed to Cleveland Workhouse

Mrs. Mary Ryan was given a heavy fine yesterday by Mayor Robert Erskine following a conviction on a charge of running a disorderly house. She was given a fine of $300 and costs and was ordered committed to the Cleveland workhouse until the fine and costs are paid.

Mrs. Ryan was charged with having operated a disorderly house at her home, located at McGill and Water Streets. With her, Mary Needham, better known as Mary Welsh, of New Castle, PA., was also arrested as was a visitor. The latter was fined $50 and costs. An alleged male visitor was also arrested, but afterwards released.

9 BOOZE, SALOONS AND PROHIBITION

Between the 1880s and before the passage of Prohibition, liquor was an important economic commodity for the Village. Liquor put Lowellville on the map as one of the rowdiest towns in Ohio. It also forced Lowellville to expand its jail, hire more police officers and hold night court to handle its 1,000 plus arrests per year. There was also an upside to the liquor related arrests, with an average fine and court costs totaling $4.85 per incident, the village was able to use the penalty money to pave its streets and make other infrastructure improvements. Those who could not pay their fines were offered overnight accommodations in the city hall jailhouse, outfitted in white coveralls and given the opportunity to work off their fines by cleaning up the streets in the morning!

There are various accounts that place the number of saloons in the village between nine and twenty-two. Whatever the actual number, these saloons made Lowellville a mecca for visitors from Struthers, East Youngstown (present day Campbell, OH) and New Castle, P.A. The peak of business for Lowellville's booze occurred beginning in 1911 when Struthers and all of Lawrence County P.A voted to go dry.

Between the late 1890s and 1915 there were a number of heated elections between the "wet" and "dry" voters. The "wets" being those who opposed something known as "local option" and the "drys" being those who supported it. Local option would allow a political subdivision to elect to prohibit the sale or serving of alcohol.

The Temperance Movement was active in Lowellville from the 1880s until the passage of prohibition, they supported abstinence from drinking alcoholic beverages. Supporters of temperance wore white ribbons which lent to the nickname "white ribboners". Although Lowellville had a strong contingent of "white ribboners" it had more of those who did not want to see the village dry up!

Here is an article about how the celebration of the defeat of local option may have contributed to the death of a local saloon keeper...

The Cleveland Leader *(Cleveland, OH) published on February 25, 1895:*

DIED WHILE CELEBRATING

Pompeo Pompoco, a Lowellville saloon keeper, died suddenly last night. During the day an election was held in the village as to whether liquor should be sold or not. The contest was very exciting between the "wets" and the "drys". Pompoco taking an active part in securing votes for the wets. When it was announced the "wets" had carried the day, Pompoco was very jubilant over the result, and while engaged in celebrating fell dead. He leaves a wife and six children.

It was not until 1920 that women across the US were given the right to vote in all elections, however in 1894 the state of Ohio passed legislation to permit women to vote in school board elections. In this article from 1895, Lowellville women offered to leverage their newly gained right in order to find a way to shut down the saloons ...

The Youngstown Vindicator *(Youngstown, OH) published on March 7, 1895:*

LOWELLVILLE WOMEN MAKE A BID FOR VOTE

About thirty of the women of Lowellville met yesterday afternoon and formulated the following request:

The women of Lowellville who desire to close the saloons, ask the men to nominate anti-saloon men for the council and Bible men for the school board, promising on their part to vote for the Bible men and to work as a unit to help elect the entire ticket. Otherwise each woman will be free to vote as she pleases, or stay at home.

Perhaps this man, John Crow, helped fuel the village's temperance supporters by his bad behavior...

The Youngstown Vindicator *(Youngstown, OH) published on December 22, 1898:*

BAD MAN
Raised a Disturbance on a P. & L. E. Train - Was Arrested

On the oath of Constable Willis Collins, of Lowellville, Justice Thomas Thursday morning, issued a warrant for the arrest of John Crow, an employee of the Mary Furnace of that village.

On December 20, it is alleged, Crow boarded passenger train No. 16, and that at a point between Struthers and Lowellville, he became disorderly, gave vent to a stream of foul and indecent language that would have done credit to the worst type of degenerate. There were a number of ladies in the car at the time. Crow also boldly challenged any or all passengers to a fist fight. The matter was referred to officials of the company who will prosecute Crow.

The warrant was turned over to Constable Collins, who will bring Crow to this city this afternoon. He will probably be given a hearing this evening.

Here is the follow-up article about John Crow, it provides a little more detail about his "bad boy" behavior and his punishment ...

The Youngstown Vindicator *(Youngstown, OH) published on December 23, 1898:*

DISGRACEFUL SCENE
Was That Created by John Crow – He Was Drunk

John Crow, of Lowellville, who created what Assistant Superintendent Davis, of the Pittsburgh & Lake Erie railroad, alleges was the most disgraceful scene ever witnessed on that company's trains was fined $3 and the costs by Justice Thomas Thursday evening.

Crow was arrested by Constable Collins, of Lowellville, on a warrant issued by Squire Thomas, charging him with creating a disturbance, using obscene language and provoking a fight. When arraigned in court Crow, who is an employee of the Mary Furnace, pleaded guilty. He also pleaded drunkenness as an excuse for his behavior.

In speaking of the affair, Superintendent Davis said Crow got on train No. 16 at Youngstown and that although there were a number of ladies in the coach, Crow made an indecent exposure of his person and, when remonstrated with, began cursing the inmates of the car in a most disgraceful manner and offered to fight the entire list of passengers. No less than five complaints were received by the company against the actions of Crow.

After submitting his plea, Crow pleaded for mercy, and at the request of the company's representative he was let off with the above named fine, which he paid promising to be good in the future.

When ladies could not convince their husbands to stop drinking, they decided that suing the saloons who provided their husbands with liquor would perhaps be more successful....

The Youngstown Vindicator *(Youngstown, OH) published on July 3, 1899:*

SUITS AGAINST SALOONS

Mrs. Sadie Wymer, wife of John Wymer, of Lowellville, has filed petitions in common pleas court against two saloon keepers of that place, for alleged selling of liquor to her husband, after being notified by the plaintiff not to do so.

The defendants to the actions are Thomas Dempsey and Steve Rushnock. This makes four suits brought against Lowellville saloon keepers inside of the past few weeks, under the state law, which makes it an offense to furnish liquor to a blacklisted person. The plaintiff wants $200 in damages in each case, and her interests are being looked after by Attorney Swanston.

Here is another story about a wife suing the saloons ... imagine if these ladies had prevailed in court and other ladies in town "got on the wagon" so to speak ... I think there would have been a lot of rich women in Lowellville!

The Youngstown Vindicator *(Youngstown, OH) published in January 25, 1906:*

LIQUOR DEALERS
Sued for Damages Alleged As a Result of Their Selling Liquor to Mr. Weaver

Mrs. Ellen Weaver, by her attorney, Frank Jacobs, has brought suit against several liquor dealers in Lowellville charging them with having sold liquor to her husband after being told and warned not to do so. The defendants are Michael Douglas, Richard Burke, and a dealer named Sylvester. Damages in the amount of $5,000 is asked from each.

The plaintiff alleges that she had repeatedly warned the saloonists not to furnish her husband, Nicholas Warner, with intoxicants, but in spite of said warnings they continued to sell him liquor, causing him to become a drunkard and making him a wreck. The usual allegations of lost positions, failure to provide for his family on account of his drunken habits, etc., are made in the petition, which was filed this afternoon.

Historical Footnote: I transcribed this article exactly as published and noticed that the wife is Mrs. Ellen Weaver and the husband is Nicholas Warner. Either there was a printing error, or this couple used different last names, which was a bit unusual in 1906.

An interesting letter published in **The Youngstown Vindicator** *(Youngstown, OH) on May 22, 1909 from a "Lowellville Citizen" asking voters to vote Mahoning County dry. Keep in mind this was during the "Temperance Movement" when the Anti-Saloon League was very strong in Ohio and there was a group of Lowellville citizens who were strong supporters of temperance. I have to say I am impressed at all the number crunching this person did without the use of a calculator and his creative accounting. Rest assured, although most of Mahoning County went dry a few years later, Lowellville, however, was one of the "lucky ones" and retained its numerous saloons!! The end though for the village saloons came finally with the passage of prohibition in 1919, and Lowellville became "dry", or at least it seemed to be dry.*

WHAT BOOZE COSTS THE PEOPLE OF LOWELLVILLE

Citizen of that Village Shows in Plain Figures How Saloon Keepers There Can Afford to Buy Valuable Real Estate, Stocks and Bonds, with 320 Men at Their Command Who "Cough Up" $342.51 a Piece As the Annual Price of "Personal Liberty" – A Bad Situation Plainly Portrayed By One Who Has Preferred to Conduct His Investigations at Home

A citizen of Lowellville, where they have "Personal Liberty" on tap in nine different parts of the village, has compiled a few facts on the tax phase of the saloon issue which are of general interest to the taxpayers of Mahoning county.

He speaks of investments made by the Lowellville saloonkeepers in real estate, stocks, bonds, etc. It is easy to see how such investments are possible for the saloonkeepers – but wonders if those "personal liberty" loving patrons don't squeal at the endless drain which these investments make on their own payrolls.

The saloonkeepers' victims are evidently paying the freight in Lowellville, as they are doing everywhere else. When will these 224 men in Lowellville wake up and figure out how long they would be making some good investment on their own book if they were able to keep their $312, instead of donating that sum annually to the saloon keeper, who gives them worse than nothing in return. The Lowellville citizen writes as follows:

"There are nine saloons in Lowellville and their expenses figured at a minimum are as follows: License, $9,000; nine bartenders at $12 a week, $5,616; board for the same at $20 a month, $2,160, rent at $25 per month, $2,700, heat $578; light, $1080; internal revenue, $225; sundries, such as broken glassware, furniture, etc.. $900; living expenses of proprietors and families, $9000; total actual expenses of the saloon, $31,259, which must come over the bar in cold cash. AS A PROFIT, before the saloon makes a profit for its owner.

"The saloonkeepers swear by all the saints in the calendar they do not make enough to exceed 40 per cent profit. If such be the case $31,259 must be the 40 per cent profit they make to be able to exist, or in other words, they must sell $78,148 worth of liquor for cash to pay their expenses. The saloonkeepers of Lowellville, judging from their investments in real estate and in stocks of different corporations, must make an average profit of at least $1,000 per year each or a total of $9,000 for which they must sell liquor to the value of $22,500 making a grand total of $100,648, which is handed over the bar each year in cold cash, and from which the tax payers of Lowellville receive back in taxes the stupendous sum of $3,600.

"At last election there were in the neighborhood of 340 voters in Lowellville. But give the saloon the best of it. Say there are 400 men in the village, and you have it that each man must pay $251.60 per year toward support of the saloon as HIS share of the taxes the saloonkeeper pays. But look a little further and you will find at least 20 per cent of the 400 do not spend a cent in the saloons, leaving 320 men to pay the $100,686 or $341.51 each.

"Now go still further and you will find 30 per cent of the 320 do not spend to exceed $5 a month or in other words, ninety-six $5-a-month men spend $5,760 leaves $94,888 to be paid by 234 men or $423 each. Then again, the saloonkeeper will say, "but my transient trade!" Well, allow $25,000 for the transient trade and we will still have a balance of $69,888 to be paid by 224 men or $312 each. Who are these 321 men? Are they the professional and business men of Lowellville or are they the laborers? And are not some of the latter who are the steadiest customers of these nine saloons the very men who are at present shouting, "don't take away my personal liberty and raise the taxes on my little home?"

"Now, Mr. Laborer, don't you think you are paying a pretty stiff tax at present in that $312 you are handing to the saloonkeeper every year, or does that amount just go to purchase your "personal liberty"? As to the personal liberty end of it, don't you think if you keep on taking the regulation amount of liquor into your stomach, the liquor will in time take away your actual personal liberty? In other words, will it not make you its slave through the uncontrollable appetite you will acquire? Think it over some morning when you have that lovely brown taste in your mouth and a head which you must handle with great care. Just strike a trial balance and see if you are not on the wrong side of the "bar".

"Think it over. I am under the impression that if every man who takes a drink of liquor, or who is a frequent visitor of the saloon would sit down in some secluded spot and review the sights he has seen all too many times right here in Lowellville he would be appalled. Young men, boys you might say, with glassy and staring eyes, pallid features and uttering in the foulest oaths, staggering away to some sink to vomit up the poison which the young and untutored stomach can no longer retain. Pleasant sight, isn't it? Heaps of "personal liberty" there. You, father, with sons just entering manhood's estate, do you wish others to make the same slighting remarks regarding your sons as you have heard, no doubt, made many times about the sons of other fathers?

"Get right on this question, men. Vote dry. Talk dry, even if you do take an occasional drink, or many of them. It will show the community that your heart is in the right place, even if your habits and stomach are a little to the bad. You may have to stand the jibes and taunts of the saloonkeeper and his kind, but in a year or so the tide will turn and you will be able to look back and say, "I am a sober man. My eyes are clear. My nerves do not require a bracer of poison in the morning. My stomach does not rebel at the sight of breakfast, and I am proud to say that I helped to put old Mahoning dry."

A CITIZEN OF LOWELLVILLE

A little quip about Lowellville in **The New Castle News** *(New Castle, PA) published on September 6, 1911:*

Drunkenness has increased eight per cent in London this past year. Lowellville, O. can beat that record to a frazzle.

I always thought that you saw "pink elephants" from drinking too much …

The New Castle News (New Castle, PA) published on November 11, 1911:

With no booze, Lowellville would probably vegetate instead of becoming the breeding place of green elephants, pink rats and other zoological monstrosities.

Interesting article that describes the liquor trade and corresponding arrests in Lowellville in the early Spring of 1913:

The New Castle News *(New Castle, PA) published on April 4, 1913:*

WET HEADQUARTERS FOR NEW CASTLE
Large Quantities of Liquid Refreshments Re-Shipped at Lowellville

March was the record month in the village in the number of arrests made and lodging supplied. The arrests totaled 119 and the lodging 110, which exceeds by a considerable number any previous record. According to the police, New Castle, which is a dry town furnishes the greater part of the offenders in police court. The thirsty ones come to the village in droves and by the time they make the rounds of the 22 saloons, they are ready for a rest and usually pretty much "broke".

Those who apply for lodging are mostly tramps who jump off the trains passing through the village.

Since Mercer county, Pennsylvania, which includes New Castle in the dry list, Lowellville has come to assume an importance as a distributing point for all kinds of "wet goods." More than 200 cases and nearly as many kegs of beer are shipped out of the village every day with the exception of Saturday when the number is doubled for points in Mercer county.

There were two offenders before Mayor Roller Thursday morning whose financial resources totaled $3.72. One had $3.60 and the other 12 cents. The amounts were applied to their fines and they were allowed to go.

This article from **The New Castle News** *was published on December 18, 1913 after the citizens of Lowellville once again voted to stay wet, it was meant to be an insult to our little place but it actually makes me feel proud to hail from such a feisty village!*

OF COURSE

Lowellville did the expected. There was much joy before and behind the bars in the caravansaries of that proud and representative municipality of the great state of Ohio. Persons who had worked indefatigably for the moist cause stood last night in groups with one foot on the brass rail, and between gulps discussed glories of victory.

It was almost a forgone conclusion that Lowellville would go "wet". Any town that has maintained a cheerful and persevering jag for as many years as Lowellville has, is not easily to be deprived of its accustomed toddy.

Lowellville firmly refuses to be legislated into righteousness. It may be necessary for Mahoning county to give her the jag cure!

Also in the same edition of the paper were these little shorts:

Thirteen is a lucky number for some people - the suds parlor owners at Lowellville for instance. (*I think they are referring to the year 1913 when this newspaper was printed*)

So Lowellville went "wet". It has been quite sloppy for some time, so could not be dried up all at once.

As one English gentleman remarked, "It's the h'Italians who put the 'ell in Lowellville."

It seems like every few years the "White Ribboners" were trying to get rid of our saloons through local option ballots. This particular election had an 88% voter turnout which shows that the village men were very interested in the results.

The Elyria Democrat *(Elyria, OH) published on December 18, 1913:*

The village of Lowellville with a voting population of about 400, at a special election by a vote of 183 to 170 decides to retain its saloons. Several arrests were made for alleged illegal voting. The campaign was spirited and bitter, but no serious disturbances occurred.

The wet majority was considerably reduced over the last election. All Mahoning county was interested, as the result may have an influence on the proposed county election being petitioned for.

Marshal Tony Fisher seemed to be very vigilant in his quest for discovering violations of the law. In this story we learn that about the subtleties of the liquor laws of the time. Fortuitously, he had the support of the newly elected Mayor, Dr. Robert Erskine, who wanted to dry up the village.

The Youngstown Vindicator *(Youngstown, OH) published on April 28, 1914:*

CRUSADE IS BEING WAGED
At Lowellville Against the Alleged Illegal Sale of Liquor
Case on This Afternoon That is Attracting Attention - Colored Man Charged with Buying Beer

Some fine points of law are expected to crop out this afternoon at the hearing before Squire Moore of Ohio against A. and John Kloffer, wholesale liquor dealers, charged by Marshal Tony Fisher with selling liquor to one John Murray, a colored man hailing from New Castle, less than in the quantity permitted by law. The white ribboners of this village are reported to be behind in urging the prosecution of this case.

It is alleged that Murray came from New Castle last Friday night and purchased two gallons of whiskey, a pint of gin and two cases of beer, requesting that shipment be made that date over the M.V. railway. It is alleged by the defendants that Murray requested that he be permitted to carry 15 bottles of beer, a part of the purchase home with him when he was informed that the liquor could not be shipped on that Friday night. The request is said to have been granted.

With his baskets filled with beer bottles, Murray was nabbed by the village police. It is alleged that he was thrown into the lockup and refused a hearing, and that no further charge was made against him until Monday, when at the suggestion of County Prosecutor Henderson he was charged with aiding and abetting the Kloffers in making an illegal sale of liquor.

Some time ago a citizen named Kurtz, the sole support of four small children, the eldest being 13 years of age, was cast into jail on a charge of bootlegging or taking part in an illegal sale of whiskey at Jacob Wilhelm's stand. It is alleged that Kurtz purchased two gallons of whiskey, that another customer came into the Wilhelm place and wanted to buy two quarts, and was refused. Kurtz to be friendly bought an additional two quarts and in turn sold it to the man at the wholesale price, not realizing a cent, it is alleged. He was arrested by Marshal Fisher charged with bootlegging and is now in the county jail in Youngstown serving out a term of three months imposed by Mayor Erskine.

The Humane Society will be appealed to it is said, in an attempt to secure the liberty of Kurtz, whose wife is dead and his children require his protection.

Poor Nick in the article below had no chance of leniency from Mayor Robert Erskine. As noted above, Mayor Erskine had little sympathy for men who came to town to partake in the liquor the village's saloons offered or purchase wholesale booze.

The New Castle News (New Castle, PA) published December 2, 1914:

COSTLY SPREE FOR POLIUS
Finds that $100 Roll Had Dwindled to $16.50 This Morning

Nick Polius, arrested last night on a charge of drunkenness and disorderly conduct, awoke this morning to a realization of the fact that it had been a costly spree to him. When he received his money taken from his person last night, he discovered that the roll of $95 or $100 he had when he first looped upon the Lowellville variety had dwindled to $16.50. He had no idea where the remainder of his money went.

When the police got him last night and he was searched, $16.50 was all the money on his person.

"You had better let your wife keep your money when you take a desire to get drunk." the mayor suggested.

"Oh, I get everything my wife wants but do not give her money. I ain't going to give her fifteen or twenty dollars to blow in. I do all the business at our house, give her money, but know what it's for."

"Yes, but if you had given her the money yesterday, you'd have been much richer this morning," the mayor told him.

"I suppose so," said Nick as he sauntered out, bemoaning the fact that his roll of Christmas money had been sacrificed somewhere because of the effect of booze on his senses.

A consequence of having lots of drunks walking about was that it also drew opportunists like pickpockets to town.

The Youngstown Vindicator (Youngstown, OH) published on August 3, 1915:

BUSY PICKPOCKETS
Reaped Quite a Harvest in Lowellville Saturday Night

Pickpockets were busy in Lowellville Saturday night and are reported to have reaped quite a harvest. The light fingered gentry found easy picking among the crowds that frequent the saloons of the village especially on Saturday nights when lovers of the cup come in large numbers from New Castle and other dry territory in Western Pennsylvania.

Among the victims of the pickpockets was Richard McCann who reported a loss of $9, while others who lost smaller amounts made no public complaint.

∼

Here is an article that points out that the liquor laws in Ohio and the US in the early 20th century were designed to ensure that taxes were paid on liquor...

The Youngstown Vindicator *(Youngstown, OH) published on October 5, 1919:*

DEPUTY GETS DRINK, ARRESTS HOTEL MAN

Joseph Melillo, Lowellville hotel owner, was arrested by Sheriff Morris and his deputies Saturday evening after one of the deputies was served with a drink of raw raisin liquor by a bartender in the saloon of the hotel. Melillo was charged with violating the state law but a federal charge may also be made against him as no tax was paid on the liquor sold in the establishment. About ten gallons of "solid drinks" were confiscated in the raid. Most of it was recently burned raisin liquor. The bartender escaped.

Melillo was arraigned before Squire Cunningham at the jail late Saturday night. He plead not guilty and was released upon furnishing $500 bond. Hearing of the case was set for Wednesday afternoon.

Historical Footnote: *Joseph Melillo owned the ten room Hotel Caneva, which he built in 1914 on the corner of Liberty and Third Streets. His hotel still stands today and is now a nice restaurant and bar operating under the name of "Melillo's Station Grille." The illegal liquor sold was "Raisin Jack" a popular type of whiskey made from fermented raisins, sugar and cornmeal.*

10 NOTABLE CHARACTERS

In this chapter are a few of the stories of some notable characters who lived in the village or who were perhaps just passing through. These stories provide a glimpse into how everyday people spent their time, how they bickered with their fellow villagers or tried to pull off a con job.

Here is an article that describes a "gambling sport" that Lowellvillians of the late 1880s found both entertaining and for some quite profitable:

The Cleveland Leader *(Cleveland, Ohio) published on April 12, 1883:*

George Dahringer defeated George Leish in a six hour walking match at Lowellville last night for $100. Leish gave out at the last hour and left the track. Over $500 changed hands on the match.

Here is a story about a con man and horses! At least he got caught…

The Cleveland Leader *(Cleveland, Ohio) published on April 16, 1884:*

W. S. Wells, a horse jockey, was arrested today and lodged in jail on a charge of obtaining money under false pretenses, at the instance of M. Book, a landlord at Lowellville, this county. Wells came to the hotel two weeks ago, representing that he was buying horses, and each day visited the country and notified farmers to bring their horses to Lowellville yesterday, and he would purchase them for shipment to New York. Upon his representation that he had $5,000 in the banks here, he secured a loan from Book and ran a board and bar bill of $60. Yesterday, the village of Lowellville was swarming with farmers with horses that they expected to sell to Wells, but he was not to be found. Today he was arrested here (Youngstown), and lodged in jail to await a hearing.

Sometimes life is stranger than fiction ...

The Youngstown Vindicator (Youngstown, OH) on August 2, 1899:

CRAZY MEN
Succeed in Making Tuesday Night Hideous at the County Jail
Strange Hallucinations

The inmates of the county jail were unable to sleep on Tuesday night owing to the actions of two crazy men confined to the institution. Francis Nessle of Lowellville was the principal offender and he made the night hideous with his unearthly yelling. The poor unfortunate was laboring under the hallucination that he was a river boat pilot, and that the boat that we was guiding was beset with all the dangers known to river navigation. First the boat was going to collide with rocks in midstream, then he feared the craft he was master of was floating over the falls of Niagara, and so it went on for hours, while the crazy man tugged with his iron bed in an effort to steer clear of the awful fate his tortured mind pictured was awaiting him and the passengers in his charge. Finally, his imagination changed, and then he began to wrestle with the mattress on his bed. He accused it of being a woman armed with a knife and the faster he disarmed her the more deadly were the weapons she produced. After keeping this up all night Nessle, finally exhausted, ceased to rave any more.

The second crazy man is colored and his name is Jerry Smith. He was brought over from Jefferson Tuesday by Sheriff O. M. Parker of Ashtabula county. Smith, at one time was employed by Dan Smeltz, imagined he had murdered his wife and had buried her body in his backyard. He could not be comforted and his wailings were pitiful in the extreme. He could not be induced to go to bed last night but stood for hours in a corner of the jail. Sheriff Parker who arrived here last evening did not return to Jefferson until Wednesday morning.

Historical Footnote: *Francis was a bachelor who was born on February 21, 1871* *in Lowellville, Ohio. He was the son of D. T. and Olive Nessle. In the 1900 census his occupation is shown as painter, not a River Boat captain. Because I was able to find him back in Lowellville and working at the time of the 1900 census, it appears that he did not spend much time in jail after this incident.*

This is a story about the Superintendent of Lowellville schools who was charged with abusing his students. The case against him was eventually dropped. H.H. Bowers served for nearly six years as Superintendent in Lowellville Schools. In 1898, a year after this story was published he went on to become the Superintendent of Girard Schools. Initially he was highly respected by the village, however, in later years his life took an awful turn when he took his own life at the age 41 in 1904. He left behind a wife and two sons ages 14 and 6. His story of decline unfolds in the articles below.

The first article was published in **The Youngstown Vindicator** *(Youngstown, OH) on May 11, 1897:*

Prof. H. H. Bower, Mrs. Bower, Misses Daisy Parsons, Pearl Houston, Alice Allshouse are to be employed as teachers in Lowellville public schools for the coming year. Every patron of the school is was very anxious, that Prof. Bower should be returned, as they well know the standing of our schools and the rapid progress that the pupils have made. This will make his fifth year as superintendent, and no teacher ever manifested greater interest in the welfare of the children in general. The instruction is so thorough and practical that the pupils know and understand what they have been studying, which prepares for life's great battle. Under his management, we can feel assured that our schools will be kept abreast of the times and in order to see the work done during the year, every parent should attend the closing exercises of the school.

The second article detail the abuse charges…

The New Castle News *(New Castle, PA) published on January 19, 1898:*

TROUBLES OF A TEACHER
He is Summoned Before the Court for Abusing His Pupils

Everett Carlon by his next friend, Chauncey Meeker, has commenced suit in common pleas court at Youngstown against H. H. Bowers, asking damages in the sum of $3,000. Bowers is one of the teachers in Lowellville schools, and is now before a grand jury charged with assault upon a number of his scholars. Carlon alleges that Bowers abused his children in a most brutal and inhuman manner in his chastisement of them for alleged misconduct while attending his school.

And finally here is an excerpt from **The Youngstown Vindicator** *(Youngstown, OH) published on September 22, 1904 about his life and death:*

To the people of the Mahoning Valley the death by suicide of Prof. Bower came as a great shock. He was known to be a man of fine physical power and an untiring worker both in the school room and in the community ... He was generally regarded as one of the most efficient men in Girard. He has the rare faculty of inspiring in the young the ambition to be great teachers and the records of the county examiners will show that his schools sent out more teachers than any other similar schools in Eastern Ohio... He gave his life unselfishly to his chosen work, always methodical. For several months he showed signs of nervous collapse. He later become despondent and on September 18 took his own life at the home of his mother. He seemed to realize the nature of his ailment and said to his wife a few days before, "I would like to give this message to my young friends; 'Don't work too hard."

While researching Lowellville, I came across the name of an early Lowellville Constable named Willis Collins, who was a member of Lowellville's police force from the late 1890s into the turn of the century. Considering the demographics of Lowellville, I just made the assumption that he was white. You can imagine my surprise when I read two articles describing him as "colored". Willis Collins lived with his wife Mary and their three children. As a police officer and local barber, he was well respected and was characterized in one article as a "shrewd" colored man. His son, William Foster Collins, settled in Youngstown and followed in his father's footsteps and served as a Youngstown City police officer in the 1940s.

Here is an article, published on July 2, 1902 in **The New Castle News** *(New Castle, PA) that describes Lowellville's early police force and the need for uniforms to help them do their jobs more effectively:*

WARNED REGARDING LOWELLVILLE'S POLICE

Lowellville now has a uniformed police force, and sports from across the Pennsylvania line should be careful how they conduct themselves when they enter the quiet and law-abiding town of Lowellville, says the *Youngstown Telegram*.

W.S. Baker, marshal of the town is now called the chief of police of Lowellville, and Constable Willis Collins is known as the town detective. Both are arrayed in blue suits and brass buttons and look quite metropolitan. This change was brought about by the action of the generous citizens of the village.

Messrs. Baker and Collins are as brave as any officers that live. They have preserved the peace of Lowellville and kept the village free from crooks for years. But they worked under a great disadvantage in one respect. Foreigners, who are used to the gorgeously dressed "coppers" of Europe, have a mortal fear of a uniform. An officer in plain clothes excites no awe in their hearts. Owing to this peculiarity Messrs. Baker and Collins have many times been compelled to club foreigners and have several times been in great danger themselves because the former had no idea that the two were officers. Had they had uniforms on, arrests could have been made without bloodshed.

For these reasons and on account of the good work they have done, the citizens of Lowellville raised money and bought the two officers brand new uniforms and now Lowellville has a police force of her own.

Historical Footnote: *Willis Collins' barber shop, which was located on Liberty Street, was one of the businesses lost in the big February 1917 fire. After suffering this financial hardship he left the Mahoning Valley and moved to Gary, Indiana.*

This guy could be the "Darwin Award Winner" for 1910. The tongue in cheek Darwin Awards are named for Charles Darwin and his theory of evolution that only the strong and smart survive and those that are neither smart or strong, do things that take them out of the evolutionary gene pool, such as this fellow.

Also I doubt the reference to "blackhands" was meant to be a pun, but it in this case it sure was.

The Plain Dealer *(Cleveland, OH) published on December 26, 1910:*

DROPS BOMB, HAND GOES
Italian Tries to Scare Dancers With Threat to Drop Explosive and Makes Good

Paul Trunossi, an Italian of Lowellville, was the victim of his own folly late Saturday night and as a result his right hand was blown off by a bomb. Trunnosi appeared at a dance hall in Lowellville armed with a dangerous looking bomb which he threatened to drop and blow up the building. The dancers fled and had barely reached the outside when they heard a terrific explosion. Trunnosi made good on his threat.

Trunnosi had dropped the bomb while attempting to juggle it he said. His right hand was blown off and he sustained several cuts to the head and body. Trunnosi was taken to the city hospital. He says he found the bomb and merely wanted to have some fun in the dance hall. Trunnosi, is from Hillsville, a hotbed for blackhands.

I included this short story because it really made me smile imaging these cute little fellows boarding the street car and doing their best to earn some change.

The New Castle News *(New Castle, PA) published on October 30, 1911:*

Two little Italian boys reap a rich harvest on the Mahoning Valley street car line between Youngstown and Lowellville. One is 12 and the other is 7 years of age. They both play the violin and they amuse passengers by playing on the train from Youngstown to Lowellville and back. After each selection, the little fellow passes his cap down the aisle and he is generally rewarded by a generous number of nickels and dimes.

Feeding the chickens can be a dangerous task when your neighbor is a nut case ...

The New Castle Herald *(New Castle, PA) published on March 29, 1915:*

GIRL IS HACKED ON THE HEAD BY AXE
Nellie Spender of near Lowellville injured – result of a quarrel

Charged with hacking the head of Nellie Spender, 13, daughter of Frank Spender, with an axe Friday evening, Stephen Chaerock was arrested by Marshal Tony W. Fisher, Saturday. The girl, while not in danger of her life, is said to be suffering severely from the long gash which she received over the right temple.

The alleged cutting affray started as the result of a quarrel between

Chaerock and Spender. The former was angry because he said Spender's daughter feeds the chickens belonging to the families and drives Chaerock's away from the food. It is said that Chaerock become loud and was ordered out of the house. He picked up an axe and while the girl was trying to take it away from him, he struck her over the head with it. She was attended by Dr. Paul B. Smith.

The Spender and Chaerock families both live in the same house, which is a double one. The homes of the parties are about one mile south of Lowellville.

And here is another story about neighbors not getting along, but this time its poor Bossy, a cow, that was the target of the neighbor's wrath ...

The New Castle Herald *(New Castle, PA) published on July 24, 1914:*

POOR BOSSY IS FED ON POISON
And Steve Ritz, Lowellville Foreigner, is Charged With Serving the Piece de Resistance

That the big things of life often have small beginnings was brought home to Steven Ritz, a young Polander of Lowellville, yesterday, when he was locked in the village jail for the night, and now, as he doefully looks back over the events of the last few weeks, he traces his arrest directly to the mooing of an invalid cow.

Feeling Strained

For some time the feelings between Steve and Mary Yonatzko, a neighbor, were strained, although his family and hers had formerly been the best of friends. As the breach widened, there were criminations and recriminations, then the climax came when a cow belonging to Mary suddenly became mysteriously ill and with eyes turned forlornly heavenward, bellowed aloud its appeal for help. Mary answered the call with all human kindness and found Bossy walking the fields with that restlessness of a man who had been eating over-ripe lobsters, or a boy who had partaken of a peck of green apples without enough salt to take out the aches.

Noting the symptoms, Mary at once jumped to the conclusion that her favorite had been poisoned, and with Burns-like deduction, decided that no one else but Steve would plan such a covert attack. Next came a hurried call to New Castle for a veterinary to relieve Bossy's pain, and at the same time a shout for the police to haul Steve off to jail.

Steve Denies

Steve, however, strenuously denies any dastardly attempt on the life of the cow, and declares he knows nothing at all of the quantity of lye said to have been found in the shady nooks where Bossy wont to ruminate. He nevertheless was brought before Mayor Robert Erskine yesterday on a charge of disturbance, all of which revolved about that first faint mooing, and after telling his story, was fined $10 and costs, or in all $19.75, since much technical evidence was necessarily introduced. Not having the money, he is obliged to spend a good part of his summer in jail while Bossy, now fully recovered from her "tummy ache", is peacefully switching flies in the meadow near her mistress' home.

John W. Shaffer, a prominent citizen, almost asphyxiated himself by letting his car run in a closed garage. In 1916 automobiles were still a bit of new technology and he probably had no idea that running a car in a garage could be so dangerous…

The New Castle News *(New Castle, PA) published on February 9, 1916:*

SHAFFER IS GASSED BY AUTOMOBILE
Accident Nearly Costs Life of Limestone Co. Superintendent
Very Unusual in Character
Started Engine of Machine in a Closed Garage and Soon Toppled Over

J.W. Shaffer, a superintendent of the Mahoning Limestone Company quarry near Lowellville, O. and well known in the New Castle area is suffering from an unusual ailment which each automobile owner ought to know about, he being gassed from the exhaust of his automobile in a closed garage. While his family were getting ready to go out driving with him he went into the garage closing the door after him.

In order to have the machine properly warmed up when his family were ready, he started the engine, after which time he began to repair a leaking tire. In a short time he felt dizzy but attributed it to his bending down to the wheel. He straightened up for a few minutes, then bent down to work at the tire again.

In a short time he became deathly sick and fell to the floor, but managed to crawl to the door, raised himself up and opened it, then fell unconscious in the doorway. After a time the fresh air revived him somewhat and he endeavored to go back into the garage and stop the engine, which he succeeded in doing, but fell again to the floor unconscious.

His wife found him there, and with the aid of a gentleman, who with his wife, is rooming with Mr. Shaffer, he was carried into the house and Dr. Badal of Lowellville was called, who worked with him for several hours.

In falling Mr. Shaffer badly injured his back by falling against a box that was on the floor. Mr. Shaffer is still confined to his bed and will be for some time. In almost all cases of this kind, it has resulted in death.

There are so many small garages that are kept tightly closed, that makes it very easy for someone to have a similar experience as Mr. Shaffer has had, with a very great possibility of fatal results.

Historical Footnote: John Wesley Shaffer was born in Bessemer, Pennsylvania on January 26, 1881 and started his career working on the Pittsburgh and Lake Erie Railroad as the tracks were being laid in the early 20th century. He then went on to work at Carbon Limestone quarry where he "greased cars". He moved up to the position of timekeeper. After a few years, he then went to work at the Mahoning Valley Limestone company where in 1912 he rose to the position of Superintendent. It was during this time that the incident with the car occurred. In 1920, he suffered a nervous breakdown and resigned his position as Superintendent. After he recovered, he secured a job as foreman at the Johnston Quarry and worked there from 1920 until 1935. His last job was at Lowellville High School where he worked as a custodian from 1935 until he retired in 1952. He and his wife Charlotte had one son, John who was born in 1910. On February 19, 1961 he passed away at age 80. He had lived at 106 E. Wood Street in Lowellville for many years.

11 CELEBRATIONS

The residents of Lowellville loved to celebrate - whether it was a national holiday like the Fourth of July, a religious holiday or other civic event. This chapter provides a glimpse of some of the early celebrations and how sometimes the most noble efforts of the organizers were wrecked by the actions of a few bad characters. The 1904 street fair was one of those celebrations that was intended to bring good attention to the village but actually had the opposite effect!

Lowellville's most well-known celebration, the Mt. Carmel Society's festival which is always held in July, has been going strong for over 120 years and its Baby Doll Dance and fireworks continue to draw thousands of spectators each year. The very first officially organized Mt. Carmel Society celebration was held on July 16, 1895 however the feast day had been celebrated in Lowellville as early as the 1880s.

Here is how Memorial Day, originally known as Decoration Day, was celebrated back in 1884. It was an all-day event. Note that the Civil War is referred to as the "late rebellion". That description certainly lets you know that this was written by a "Yankee" newspaper. Originally Memorial Day was celebrated on the last day of May rather than the last Monday as it is today. So this event took place on a Friday. Finally keep in mind, there were no cars in 1884 and the folks in this story had to travel by horse and buggy or on foot between all of these cemeteries!! No wonder it was an all-day affair.

The New Castle News *(New Castle, PA) published on June 4, 1884:*

DECORATION DAY AT LOWELL
Lowellville, Ohio, June 2, 1884

The program laid out by Reno Post, of this place, was carried out to the letter Friday. The Post organized at 8:30am and left at once for Hillsville cemetery, accompanied by the brass band, of this place. On arriving at the out-skirts of that village, the Post was met by a number of citizens and presented with two beautiful banners made by the Misses Ripple of that place. Proceeding a short distance to the cemetery we found one hundred children in line from the three schools of Hillsville, Quakertown, and Miller's district, under the supervision of Dr. Porter, each school being accompanied by their teachers, Miss Davis, Miss Nevin and Miss Henly. Each scholar carried a beautiful bouquet which they presented to the members of the post as they passed through their lines. At the cemetery the decorating ceremonies were gone through with the graves of the sixteen comrades decorated. Eloquent addresses were made by Rev. Kirk of Hillsville, and Rev. Taylor of Westfield.

We were given a hearty welcome by the people of Hillsville. Great credit should be given to Dr. Porter for his assistance, and also to the choir for the singing rendered on the occasion, and to Misses Williams for a beautiful cross and star of choice flowers.

We then proceeded to the Mahoning church cemetery, where we were met by the school of that place under the management of Miss Lizzie Thompson, who presented us with a quantity of beautiful flowers for decorating the graves of 13 of our comrades whose last resting places are in that beautiful cemetery. After the unusual ceremonies, Comrade Watson offered an apology for the absence of Comrade Johnson, who was to have made an address at that place. On invitation Comrade Watson made a short but eloquent address, such as he can make on short notice.

We then proceeded to Lowellville and dismissed until 2:30 pm, when we again organized and accompanied by the band, and a number of citizens we visited the grave of Lieut. Nessle, which was strewn with flowers; from there to Lowellville cemetery, where the full G.A.R. ceremonies were observed. We then proceeded to the U.P. Church and listened to an address by T. J. Roller who paid a glowing tribute to the soldiers of the late rebellion. After the address the song, "We drank from the same canteen" was sung by William Roller, assisted by the choir and was rendered beautifully. We then returned to the G.A.R. Hall and dismissed with feeling we had but done our duty to our fallen comrades. -- One of the Boys.

The Mt. Carmel Society was chartered by the state of Ohio in 1895. They held their very first "official" Mt. Carmel Feast on July 16, 1895. There were two articles published about the very first festival. The first article below describes the festivities that took place – a mass, a parade and fireworks – all of which continue today. The second article, however, reported on a ruckus that almost marred the first celebration.

The Youngstown Vindicator *(Youngstown, Ohio) published on July 17, 1895:*

LADY OF MT. CARMEL
Italians Feast Being Celebrated at Lowellville Today

The Italians of this vicinity are engaged today in celebrating the feast of Our Lady of Mt. Carmel. Combined with the religious exercises are patriotic observances, and the stars and stripes are carried side by side with their religious emblems.

The celebration is taking place this year at Lowellville, and delegates are present from Youngstown, Sharon, Niles, Warren and New Castle, Beaver Falls, and many of the smaller places of this section. The delegation from this city (Youngstown) numbered about 100, and were accompanied by the Catholic band.

The exercises at Lowellville consist of high mass at 11 o'clock, celebrated by an Italian priest, and a parade at 12 o'clock. The afternoon will be devoted to social pastimes, and a grand display of fireworks takes place in the evening.

A place for the celebration next year will be selected today.

The festival brought to town other Italian immigrants from as far away as Warren, Ohio which, in 1895, was quite a distance to travel. The feast was of great social importance to the Mahoning Valley's Italian immigrants for it was a chance to see old friends and to socialize. It was also a place to show off one's pretty girl and it was just this occasion that led to quite an affray.

A "dusky maiden from the East End" found herself sought after by two men. This is how the object of two men's affections was described in the newspaper. In the press of the day, it was not uncommon to refer to a "non-anlgo" person as "dusky". The "East End" is present day Campbell, Ohio or known then as East Youngstown. The name of the pretty girl was not recorded by the newspaper, but the names of her two admirers were. The two men were identified as "Lorenzo Lorentz" and "Rock Fatlitz", its clear that the reporter had difficulty reporting Italian surnames, as Fatlitz is in no way possible

Italian and so "butchered" that determining the real surname is near impossible.

SHOT AT HIM
A Jealous Italian Tries to Kill a Rival Yesterday
Bullets Go Wide of the Mark
An Affray at Lowellville During the Celebration That Was Held There

The Italians of this vicinity yesterday afternoon celebrated the feast of the Lady of Mt. Carmel in Lowellville, returning home in the evening. With the celebration, which is of a religious and social nature and which is similar to a Fourth of July observance, was coupled a shooting affray, which might have resulted seriously, but turned out otherwise, as Lorenzo Lorentz has only a hole in his hat to remind him of what he is said to have said to his countryman, Rock Falitz of Niles.

A dusky maiden of the East End, but whose name could not be ascertained, was sought after by both Lorentz and Falitz, and both are said to be deeply in love with the Italian maid. It seems that Falitz secured her attention more than his opponent Lorentz, and as the two promenaded about in their gay, fantastic colors, Lorentz is said to have remarked: "Dago, there goes the dirty dago," which the Italians claim means dog or worse yet in their country. It is considered a great insult by them and Falitz was quick to resent it.

He immediately pulled a "bull dog" revolver from his pocket. The gun was loaded to the muzzle and he began firing at Lorentz, who, seeing Falitz so angered, began running away as fast as possible.

The first shot went through Lorentz's hat, and a second one grazed his neck and shoulder. Falitz was then interfered with by friends and prevented from what possibly might have resulted in murder. Shortly after the shooting he was locked up in Lowellville and the charge of shooting with the intent to kill placed against him. Bail offered by his Italian friends was refused.

Lorentz returned with the Youngstown party. He resides at Brier Hill and works at the furnace. Today the facts were reported to Chief McDowell and were practically the same as stated above.

Both have heretofore borne the record of being peaceful Italians and the others of their race, regret the affair particularly happening during such festivities, as they were celebrating yesterday.

Below are two articles describing a turn of the century Fourth of July celebration ... I would have loved to have seen the "fat man's race" described in the second article! And I wonder what ever happened to the village cannon mentioned in the second article?

The Youngstown Vindicator *(Youngstown, OH) published on June 23, 1900:*

BIG CELEBRATION
It Will Be Held at Lowellville on Fourth of July

Sam Schontz, the popular hotel proprietor of Lowellville, was at the head of a committee from that place who called at the **Vindicator** office this morning. Schontz says the visit to the city today was made for the purpose of a booming Fourth of July celebration to be held at Lowellville. Elaborate preparations have been made and a good program will be presented. There will be bicycle, foot, pony and tub races and, in fact, all kinds of other sports. A big fireworks display and a patriotic ball will wind up the day's celebration. The committee expects many people from surrounding towns to be present and make the event a success, and Landlord Schontz promises to see that they are all taken care of in ship-shape condition.

Another mention on June 21, 1900 in **The Youngstown Vindicator:**

The Fourth of July will be celebrated here by a morning salute from the village cannon, spreading to the breeze Old Glory, a bicycle race, foot race, fat man's race, prizes for each. Music by the band. Good hotel and boarding house accommodations, first class dinners. Fine ice cream parlors. Fireworks at night. Dance at Leish opera house.

Here is a series of articles that was published in **The Youngstown Vindicator** *(Youngstown, OH) reporting on the fabulous and I mean fabulous all out street fair that Lowellville hosted back in 1904 ... I so wish that I could have been walking the streets of the village back in October 1904:*

Published on October 8, 1904

STREET FAIR
Lowellville Will be Mecca for Pleasure Seekers This Week
Town in Holiday Dress
Long list of Premiums and Prizes Offered – Public Wedding on

Wednesday

Beginning tomorrow and throughout the remainder of the week Lowellville will be the mecca for pleasure seekers. The big street fair, through the medium of which the world is to hear of Lowellville and to become acquainted with the town's good qualities will be open tomorrow morning. This is a day of preparation for the big show. Citizens have been anticipating the event for weeks. The town is bedecked in its brightest holiday attire; the bands that will furnish music throughout the week have been riding over the trolley lines of the two valleys today advertising the fair and exhibitors have been thronging to the town and have been placing their wares where they will show to the best advantage. Housewives have been baking and preparing for a good attendance throughout the week of their country friends and relatives. Hotels, restaurants, church societies and organizations that will feed the public for a consideration, have provided for visiting thousands.

Public spirited people of the village have cleaned the streets and their door yards so that as a result the town shows off to its best advantage.

A long list of premiums have been offered as prizes for the best of everything from a pretty woman to a glass of jelly.

In addition to music, the pretty town, the prizes and the great crowds, other attractions and features of entertainment are offered. A balloon ascension and parachute leap every evening, a marvelous tight-wire performer and the slide for life, several times each day, fireworks after dark, cakewalks and colored dancers, a vaudeville show, a public wedding on Wednesday, ball games, dances and special illumination of the streets of the town are offered with a view to making the event one of the greatest shows ever held in the Mahoning Valley.

All of the railroads and the street car line expect to handle big crowds.

Also published on October 8, 1904:

GREAT CROWD
Visited and Marveled at the Wonders of the Lowellville Fair
Formal Opening Today
All Ordinances Have Been Suspended and the Village is Wide Open – The Attractions

Though the weather has been dead against us and the formal opening of the fair has been postponed by one day, yet there are more people on the streets of Lowellville than ever before in the history of the town.

This was statement yesterday afternoon of Charles Brown, proprietor of the Mahoning Valley Hotel at Lowellville, and one of the most active promoters of the street fair.

Throughout the fore part of the day yesterday the clouds hung low and an occasional drizzle discouraged those who had spent time and money for the big show. But shortly after noon the sun broke forth and the remainder of the afternoon and evening was fair. The formal opening of the fair has been continued until Wednesday but all of the open air attractions were put on, all of the little sideshows were opened, and the barkers from their elevated points of vantage spieled forth the merits of the wonders contained within the six by eight – more or less – canvases.

From the portable bandstand, moved at will from one attraction to another, the members of the Tod Post band rendered jaunty airs appropriate to the act being presented.

Water street in the little town has been converted into midway, or a pike – the latter being the more modern term. Tents and booths line each side of the street and in each something is presented for sale or some show of more or less merits presents a thrilling attraction. All of the shows are playing on a percentage, the street fair committee having refused to permit any carnival company to monopolize the show features, but giving place to all who wished to enter on the prescribed terms.

These special shows are no better than the open air exhibitions which consist of two balloon ascensions daily, the high dive, the slide for life, the wonderful boy balancer, the Bohemian jugglers and the Hindoo sword swallowers and knife throwers, etc. Good weather is all that is essential to the crowd, so the members of the committee say.

All the ordinances of the town have been suspended for a week so the town is wide open. The crowd is without restraint, yet it is orderly and good natured and most everything goes. Some of the church people are offering what discouragement they can, but they appear to be in the minority and the fair appears to be prospering without their moral support or patronage.

And a follow-up story published on October 16, 1904:

DEFICIT
Is What Lowellville Street Fair Committee Finds on the Ledger
But Town Wanted the Advertising that a Fair Would Give and It Got It

At an early hour this morning the last street lamp in Lowellville was dimmed and the curtain dropped on the great street fair of the village. The itinerant side shows presenting anything from an Oriental dance to a snake eater pulled up stakes during the evening and hide off to new fields.

The committee that had charge of the fair has balanced with the ledger and finds some deficit, but the advertising the town received has compensated for the cost of the game.

"We gave the people too much for their money," was the statement made yesterday evening by one of the committee in explanation of the deficit. "We had too many free attractions. All of the little shows under the canvas kicked because we kept the people too well amused outside. The representative that the shows under the canvas were sizzling hot was not sufficient attraction to bring in the business. The facts were the shows were just as tame as the usual sideshow fakes. The real entertainment was that which furnished the crowds for nothing.

"We spent too much money on the balloon ascensions, the fireworks, the high dive, the slide for life, and the many other features. The privileges brought in little and the percentage from the sideshows was nothing to speak of. Some of it was of the undesirable kind but much of it was good."

After the middle of the week none of the Youngstown gamblers, who fleeced everybody right and left at the beginning of the fair could be found within the limits of Lowellville. They were reported to have been afraid of their lives. The committee having the fair in charge declare that the gamblers operated without their consent and knowledge and that they will assist the grand jury in looking up their offenses.

Another street fair will be held in Lowellville next year, it is stated.

And here is some dirt on the street fair about a "Hoochee-Coochee" show that wasn't in the articles above!! I am sure that the "good people of Lowellville" were quite appalled by some of the entertainment.

The New Castle News (New Castle, PA) published on October 19, 1904

LOWELLVILLE FAIR COMES IN FOR CENSURE

The following is taken from the *Youngstown Telegram* of Saturday:

From the tips that have been passed around in the vicinity of Central Square on Saturday by some of the crowd from the city that attended the Lowellville Street Fair Friday night, the indications are that a much larger crowd will run out to Lowellville Saturday evening to see what's doing.

According to the tips put out about the doings at Lowellville, a "Hoochee-Coochee" show Saturday night will far surpass anything that has so far taken place there and it is said by men who have seen it, that it could be no worse and that the wonder is that the moral element of Lowellville does not take the matter in hand and put a stop to the indecent exhibitions that take place there nightly and another of which is tipped off for Saturday night that, it is said, will put to shame anything of the kind that has been attempted before. It was stated positively by one of the men in the party from the city who attended the exhibition Friday night, that two women dance without a stitch of clothing on them before a crowd of men and boys. The Mayor of Lowellville has been quoted as saying that he has seen worse dances than the one that is given at the Lowellville fair, but *The Telegram* informant has very likely forgotten more such sights than the Mayor of Lowellville ever heard of and he declared that he had never seen anything that could hold a candle to the Lowellville affair.

Many other exhibitions which do anything but reflect credit on the good people of Lowellville were recounted by the visitors. One of them expressed himself as follows: "We visited the saloons and saw two hard fights and in one a man was pretty done up. There was drinking and fighting everywhere it seemed to me. I do not think there were more than 200 people in the street where the fair was held and many of them were boys, but the element on hand was certainly taking advantage of the opportunity to have the time of its life."

Finally here is another article that describes in more detail the illegal gambling action briefly mentioned earlier. There is also a mention of the suicide of someone believed to have been swindled.

The New Castle News (New Castle, PA) published on October 19, 1904:

A LOCAL MAN LOST $235 TO GAMBLERS

Samuel Stillwagon, of this city, was "touched" for $235 at the Lowellville street fair Tuesday afternoon by crooks, who ran a gambling game, at which no one but themselves could win. Just as they were to be arrested the crooks fled, carrying off Stillwagon's coin with them.

A "pinch wheel" was used, that being a wheel of fortune device in which the operator is able to stop the indicator at a blank point, where the victim cannot win. However, Stillwagon did not know what he was up against until afterward. The wheel was located in a booth under the charge of the Youngstown gamblers.

The wheel looked good to Stillwagon, who first invested $1. He won and tried again, winning another "plunk" it seemed a case of easy money and he invested $5, when he lost. Cappers in the game also lost and the operator suggested that they double the bets. Stillwagon was game, but lost again.

This continued until he was $100 to the bad. Then the operator told him to put everything he had and if he lost all but a per cent of his losses would be returned. That was a proposition that almost any person would accept, and Stillwagon pulled out $135 more and placed it on the wheel.

There were 50 spaces marked out by little pegs about the circle in which the indicator spun and only two of these were blanks, apparently. However, the majority of the spaces were marked by buttons. When the pointer stopped at a blank space the investor lost. When it stood still, pointing at a button, the operator won. "Heads I win, tails you lose". It was a good game for the man running it.

Just as Stillwagon spun the indicator for the last time, after staking his $135, the operator qualified the statement that he would give back two for one, provided that Stillwagon won. However, this was not necessary, for the New Castle man lost.

Stillwagon then quit the game, but shortly after met George C. Brown, son of the late John B. Brown, of this city, who advised him to have the gamblers arrested for running a fake game. Acting on this advice Stillwagon went to Burgess Thomas Whitmer, of Lowellville, who told him first to return to the gamblers and demand his money back; then have them arrested if they refused.

Stillwagon did so, but did not have a chance to demand his money back, as the gamblers seized all the money in sight and fled, when they saw him approaching. They ran through the hotel and out the rear way, escaping to the Lowell inter-urban line, jumping aboard one of the cars as it was leaving the town.

The gambling scheme robbed several people Tuesday and may have led to the suicide of Harry Allshouse, of Youngstown, who late Tuesday night shot and killed himself at Struthers, after leaving the Lowellville fair. It was reported that he was a New Castle man, but this was incorrect. It was reported that Allshouse had lost $400 to the gamblers, but this was erroneous.

Here is the article about Harry Allshouse's death .

The Repository *(Canton, Ohio) published on October 12, 1904:*

SHOT HIMSELF
After Losing $400 at Street Fair Held at Lowellville

Harry Allshouse, a young man residing in Lowellville, while attending the street fair held here lost about $400. He boarded a street car and went to Struthers and on arriving at the station deliberately shot himself with a revolver, dying in a few minutes.

Historical Footnote: Harry was about 32 years old when he died. He was the son of William Allshouse and Elizabeth Armagost Allshouse. He is buried in the Lowellville cemetery near his parents.

12 COLORFUL MAYORS

Lowellville's early mayors were certainly a colorful lot of fellows, each one had a different character and we are fortunate that they were so newsworthy, for their antics provide us with some great tales.

In a series of articles in this chapter we learn about Mayor Thomas Whitmer, whose tenure as mayor seemed to be filled with opposition. He definitely earned the title "Lowellville's Fighting Mayor." He always seemed ready to fight someone on a matter he stood upon. His opponents were the members of village council, the citizens and the railroad.

Another colorful mayor was John Shannon Roller, who only served two years as mayor but who made the newspapers for his antics. He had a penchant for alcohol and a leniency towards others who liked it too.

The man who succeeded him as mayor, Dr. Robert Erskine, was just the opposite. Mayor Erskine was a physician by education and practice and his goal was to see Lowellville become dry. He was known as "Dr. Bob" and was a tough by the book kind of politician who showed no leniency to those who violated village's laws.

The village council and Mayor Whitmer did not see eye to on many matters; so when a council vacancy arose, Whitmer tried his earnest to ensure he had an ally on council … but the village council had a mind of their own on the matter …

The Youngstown Vindicator (Youngstown, OH) published on January 21, 1905:

MAPES TURNED DOWN
The Lowellville Council Refused to Confirm the Mayor's Appointment

Members of the Lowellville council refuse to accept the appointment of

119

J. C. Mapes as member of the council to succeed Dan Davidson, who resigned and moved to Kentucky. At a special meeting of the councilmanic body Mapes was not recognized as a member and the meeting broke up without having accomplished anything. The next meeting will be held the first Monday in February when the matter will be fought over with renewed energy. Mayor Whitmer, president of the council, who is opposed in his administration by all members of council, claims he has the law on his side, while other members of council supported by City Solicitor L. H. E. Lowery, say the law is in conflict with the mayor's appointment.

A second article published a few days later in **The New Castle News** *(New Castle, PA) on January 25, 1905:*

A BIG RUCTION IN LOWELLVILLE COUNCIL

The Lowellville Council Chamber was the scene of considerable excitement Thursday evening. At a special meeting of Council, Mayor Whitmer announced that he had appointed and sworn into office J. C. Mapes, to succeed D. A. Davidson, who recently resigned and who left Friday for Somerset, Ky., where he will make his future home. Mapes at the last election was defeated for the office of Davidson, and who is a member of the Whitmer faction in policies. The opposition, headed by Councilmen Ashton, Williams and Johnson want Dixon McBride appointed. At the meeting Thursday evening these members refused to recognize Mapes as a member and instructed the village clerk not to call his name when the roll call was called. The mayor read several sections of the law in reference to his right to make the appointment to which the village solicitor L. H. E. Lowery, took exceptions. Council adjourned until the first Monday in February, when the matter will again be taken up.

Johnston, Ashton and Williams claim to have the legal right and that they will make the appointment at that meeting.

Mapes was, quite a number of years ago, a resident of New Castle, and has a large number of acquaintances in this city.

A month later and things were still not better between the Mayor and council.

The New Castle News *(New Castle, PA) published on February 15, 1905:*

STILL DEADLOCKED

The Lowellville council Tuesday night deadlocked again. After the session had started with Mayor Whitmer in the chair, Councilman Johnson moved for the vacancy in council be filled by the appointment of Dickson McBride. The motion was seconded and the Mayor refused to put it because he declared the vacancy on the board had been filled by his appointment at a previous meeting when he named Mr. Mapes.

Johnson then took an appeal from the chair and the chair refused to listen to it.

After considerable argument the matter was dropped by mutual consent and other matters of business were taken up.

And it seemed to get worse because the following month the police were asked to guard the March council meeting.

The New Castle News *published on March 15, 1905:*

POLICMEN STAND GUARD ON LOWELLVILLE COUNCIL

Police officers were on hand at the meeting of council at Lowellville last night, says the **Youngstown Vindicator** of Tuesday. Mayor Thomas Whitmer, who is president of the Council, called them there for the purpose of preserving order if disorder threatened to mar the serenity of the session. As compared with the strenuous meetings of the past, the session last night was a tame sample.

Both of the successors to the disputed seat made vacant by the resignation of Dan Davidson, were in attendance. Both answered to roll call and voted on measures. Their votes were recorded. Each vote counted a full vote and not half of one, as some contended should be the case where two Councilmen insist on occupying the same seat.

Mayor Whitmer, president of Council, insisted that his appointee, J. C. Mapes, had the legal rights to the seat but as he and Mr. Mapes have no inclination to be unpleasant, they will continue to hold their rights, as they see them, and will allow the other Councilmen, and their appointee, Dickson McBride, to also hold their place. Mayor Whitmer asked the supporters of McBride to go into the courts and oust Mapes if they thought McBride had the greater right. The Councilmen dropped the matter by insisting they did not wish to rush into court.

Over the next week, J.C. Mapes decided to fight for his council seat in court…

The New Castle News *(New Castle, PA) published on March 22, 1905:*

HAS REACHED COURT
The Fight in The Lowellville Council Results in Legal Action
Lowellville's Councilmanic fight jumped into the circuit court this morning, says the *Youngstown Vindicator* of Tuesday.

Attorney, John Roller, representing J. C. Mapes, whom Mayor Whitmer appointed to fill the vacancy in Council caused by the resignation of D. A. Davidson, appeared before Judges Cools, Barrows, and Lauble this morning and asked leave to file a petition in one warrants for the purpose of determining by what right Dixon McBride claims the vacant seat. McBride had been elected by Council to fill the vacancy. Council is refusing to recognize the Mayor's appointee. The Circuit Court granted leave to file the petition and set Thursday morning at 9 A.M. as the hour for hearing on the application. Mr. Roller was instructed to notify the defendants to the action and the time set for the hearing. Mr. Roller expressed the belief that Attorney L. H. E. Lowrey, solicitor of the village, will represent McBride. Council acted, in the election of McBride, on Lowrey's advice, and he will in all probability defend in Circuit Court.

The petition which Roller filed is entitled, "The State of Ohio ex. rel. J. C. Mapes vs Dixson McBride."

He sets forth that D. A. Davidson previously qualified member of the council of the village of Lowellville resigned his place on January 15, and that on January 19 Mayor Thomas Whitmer, in compliance with the law regulating such matters, appointed J. C. Mapes. It further states the case in the following words.

"The said respondent, Dixon McBride, well knowing the fact of the appointment and qualifying of this relator to the office of Councilman of said incorporated village to fill the unexpired term of Daniel A. Davidson, thereupon usurped and intruded into and has unlawfully held and exercised the office of Councilman in said incorporated village in the place and stead of Daniel A. Davidson, resigned and against the protest of this relator, J. C. Mapes and his legal and lawful right to hold and occupy the office of Councilman in accordance with his said appointment.

"Wherefore this relator prays to the court that the defendant be ousted from said office and the possession given to said relator, J. C. Mapes."

Eventually the council prevailed and Mapes was ousted, but the Mayor was still in a pretty sour mood some six months later over the incident ...

The New Castle News *published on October 18, 1905:*

LOWELLVILLE'S FIGHTING MAYOR

Mayor T. J. Whitmer of Lowellville, is again in the lime-light. Now he is after the scalps of the city solicitor of Lowellville, L. H. E. Lowry, and village clerk H. W. Williams and incidentally taking a swipe at City Solicitor S. S. Conroy of this city, says the **Youngstown Telegram**. An opportunity has come to the doughty mayor to make a little trouble for some of the men who have opposed him and who had a hand in the unseating of the mayor's favorite for a place in the Lowellville council in the Mapes-McBride fight not long ago.

Council Employed Attorneys

Mapes was the man for who the mayor fought and several times came near bleeding. Mapes was finally defeated and his opponent was made a member of the council in his stead.

In that fight, which will go down in the history of Lowellville as one of the hardest and most spectacular in its history, the mayor fought single-handed against the rest of the city council, over whose meetings it is his duty in his capacity of mayor to preside. The city council named City Solicitor L. H. E. Lowry to conduct its end of the fight and he took on the City Solicitor of Youngstown, Attorney S. S. Conroy, to assist him. They brought quo warrants proceedings to oust J. C. Mapes, the mayor's candidate, and to seat Dixon McBride, the council's candidate for the vacant chair. They won out for McBride and the mayor's candidate was ousted and McBride was seated. When the next payroll came before the council it contained one item of $25 for Attorney L. H. E. Lowry and another of $30 for Attorney S. S. Conroy, for legal services in the proceedings described.

Mayor Opposed Payment

The council took action on the payroll as a whole, ordering the payment of all bills mentioned in it. The mayor promptly and emphatically declared that he would sign the payroll, but that he desired it be distinctly understood that he wished no orders drawn for the payment of the bills of Attorneys Lowry and Conroy, on the grounds that the services, if paid for at all, should be paid for by the members of council as individuals, and not by the village. However, the mayor had signed the payroll and Village Clerk H. W. Williams went ahead and drew orders for the payment of the disputed bills, and they were paid.

And now comes Mayor Whitmer with suits in the court charging the village clerk with fraudulently issuing orders for the payment of the disputed claims and against Attorney Lowry for fraudulently receiving money to which he had no legal right and both men were arrested. Attorneys Lowry, Conroy and Village Clerk Williams had a confab with the mayor at his office at Lowellville, Tuesday evening, but as each side was obstinate in its contention that it was in the right, it was agreed to let the matter come to a hearing before Mayor Whitmer on Friday morning and to have jury trials before the mayor. Attorney Lowry and Clerk Williams gave bond for their appearance.

In 1905 the Baltimore and Ohio Railroad had a major construction project in town that caused quite an uproar in the village. Work being done by a B&O crew was causing sewage to backup into folks' basements and they were mad. They made threats against the crew foreman and in the article below a riot is described with the village fire department trying to control the Italian B&O workers with a fire hose! The scene was a bit ugly but the Italian workers were not deterred and fought back in quite a clever way against the villagers with Mayor Whitmer caught in the middle of the fray.

The Plain Dealer *(Cleveland, OH) published on March 25, 1905:*

HELD LABORERS AT BAY

Lowellville Citizens Used Water, but Italians Cut the Hose and Won the Day

Lowellville was the scene of a riot last night when citizens turned out with the fire department to interfere with the work of 100 Italians in the employ of the Baltimore & Ohio Railroad Co on the new construction through the city.

The Baltimore & Ohio filled up a stream which served as a sewer for the village and a number of cellars were overflowed. The citizens dug out the fill and when the company sent the laborers to refill it there was trouble.

The fire department with a huge stream drove off the foreigners. They were reinforced and cut the hose, winning the day.

Mayor Whitmer, who was on the side of the railroad company, and H. M. Boyle, president of the village council, clashed and there was a fight. Today an injunction was issued for the railroad company against the citizens from interfering. A council meeting was proposed in Lowellville to settle the dispute but it did not materialize.

Historical Footnote: Lowellville's riot ended with a few minor physical bruises but much bigger bruised egos. The following day, Whitmer turned himself in to the village's police headquarters to face an assault charge against Hugh Mont Boyle. However, since no one was there to arrest him, he remarked to a **Vindicator** *reporter that in his opinion that the matter had been dropped.*

John Shannon Roller may very well have been the village's most colorful mayor, even though his tenure was only one term. In fact, it was almost not a complete term! He was very well-qualified for the office of mayor as he had the distinction of previously serving as mayor for two other Ohio villages, Canfield and Washingtonville. He also had a long career in local government as the solicitor for both Youngstown and Lowellville for many years.

He moved to Lowellville after the death of his wife and practiced law in Mahoning County for over five decades. On paper his credentials could not be beat. Mayor Roller was elected mayor at the age of seventy-one, but if you think that he was a kindly little old man, you would be much mistaken.

The Harrisburg Daily Independent *(Harrisburg, PA) published on March 7, 1913:*

DISSIPATED MAYOR
Drunk Since New Year, Wanted to Kiss Preacher

Mayor John S. Roller, of Lowellville is going to get a clean shirt, a shave, some new shoes and a suit before he goes to Columbus to appear before Governor Cox, on the charge of misconduct in office, which was filed against him by the members of the village Council. He says that he has administered the office in a proper manner, and that the people who make charges against him, have nothing to say about his personal conduct.

He appeared at the village office Wednesday morning with a black eye, which he explained was the result of contact with the janitor.

The charges were filed after the Mayor had "gone forward" in a church meeting and, according to reports, had attempted to kiss the preacher. The formal charges before the Governor says that when he got drunk he detailed a policemen to watch him in the village jail. Other charges are that he has been drunk since January 1.

Roller kept his job, but his leniency towards drunks and others who broke the law caused a conflict with Patrolman Thomas Driscoll. So Driscoll would find ways to get around Roller when it came to enforcing the law...

The New Castle News *(New Castle, PA) published on July 7, 1913:*

RAID CARNIVAL AT LOWELLVILLE
Police Officer Fired By Mayor Because of Arrest of Gamblers

A deputy sheriff from Youngstown raided the street carnival at Lowellville Saturday night and arrested one man charged with conducting a gambling device in violation of the law. Some days ago Officer Driscoll of Lowellville arrested two such men with the carnival company for conducting a gambling device, but the mayor of the village ordered the men released. When Driscoll protested at the action of the mayor he was removed from the force. Driscoll was then sworn in as a Deputy Constable and again made arrests, taking his prisoners this time before a Lowellville squire. Prosecutor Henderson was appealed to and declared that gambling would not be allowed, and the deputy sheriff took a hand Saturday night as stated.

With tension mounting between the Driscoll and Roller, Driscoll confronted Roller about the way Roller was handling cases, and Roller promptly fired him... however, Driscoll was not unemployed very long. He went to the Village Council who took only three minutes to decide to reinstate him!

The New Castle News *(New Castle, PA) published on July 11, 1913:*

LOWELLVILLE COP RESTORED TO JOB
Charges of Mayor Fail to Stick - Patrolman Goes Back on Duty
Tonight

Patrolman Thomas Driscoll, suspended July 4, by Mayor John S. Roller was reinstated by council on Wednesday evening. Mayor Roller preferred charges of insubordination and using profane language against Driscoll but council determined the charges were unfounded. Driscoll will return to work immediately. The verdict of not guilty was returned within three minutes after council heard the charge.

Prosecuting Attorney Henderson represented Driscoll in the case. One witness was retained by each side. The city hall was packed by curious persons who had expected sensational developments might result.

In 1914 Roller was succeeded by "dry" mayor Dr. Robert Erskine. After a few months in office, Erskine got tired of the city hall being a place for men to gather in the mornings for apparently non-village business, in this article we see how the new mayor decided to clean up city hall ...

Published in **The New Castle News** *(New Castle, PA) on July 3, 1915:*

FORMER MAYOR IS UNDER ARREST

Mayor Robert Erskine of Lowellville yesterday ordered the town marshal to clear the mayor's office and council chamber of the village of the chronic loafers and drunks who are said to have congregated in the building early each morning. The marshal was told to place the accused in the village jail at the rear of the town hall. Among those locked up on a charge of drunkeness was ex-Mayor John S. Roller of Lowellville. He was charged with being one of the loafers in the town hall.

Historical Footnote: *Dr. Erskine served only one term as mayor and was succeeded by C.J.Zuercher. Dr. Erskine was born February 8, 1854 to James and Catherine Geddes Erskine. He moved to Lowellville as a young man and started out in the mercantile business. When he was in his thirties he decided to attend medical school and became a practicing physician and was one of several doctors in the village. One of his biggest dreams was to see Pine Hollow to officially become a owned village park. His dream came true and on August 31, 1933 while walking home at 11:00 pm on Walnut Street after having just spent the day at the park dedication celebration, he dropped dead of a stroke on the sidewalk. He is buried in the Lowellville cemetery.*

ABOUT AUTHOR

Roslyn Torella grew up in a little corner of the Mahoning Valley called Lowellville, Ohio and considers herself to be the village's "self-appointed unofficial village historian". She is married to another Mahoning Valley native, Ron Reese, who has been forced to endure hearing stories about Lowellville for the last five years.

Roslyn is a graduate of Lowellville High School and Youngstown State University. Her other interests include Italian American family history research and genealogy. She is a contributing writer for *La Gazzetta Italiana* and *The Hometown Journal*. She can be contacted at LowellvilleHistory@gmail.com

Made in the
USA
Lexington, KY